D1096154

AMALIENBORG

Jørgen Larsen   Thomas Larsen   Bjarke Ørsted

AMALIENBORG

GYLDENDAL

CONTENT

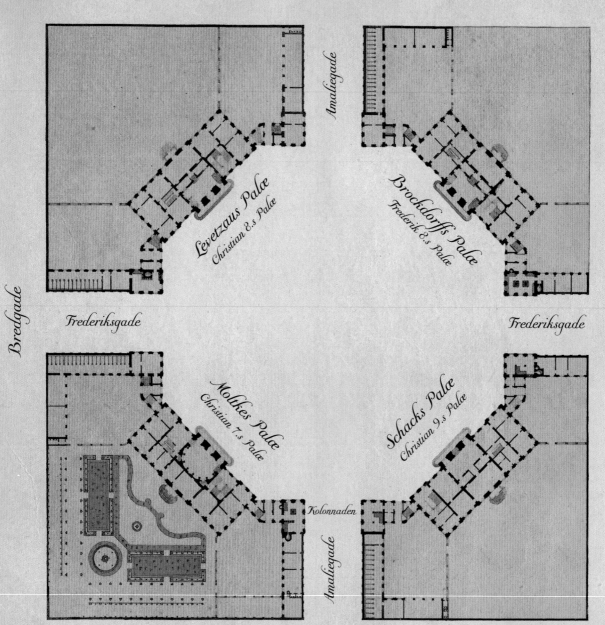

Amaliegade

Levetzaus Palæ
Christian 8.s Palæ

Brockdorffs Palæ
Frederik 8.s Palæ

Bredgade

Frederiksgade

Frederiksgade

Toldbodgade

Molthes Palæ
Christian 7.s Palæ

Schacks Palæ
Christian 9.s Palæ

Kolonnaden

Amaliegade

Preface

Upon entering the Amalienborg palace square and seeing the four palaces, most spectators will immediately sense the mastery of architect Nicolai Eigtved. But what goes on behind the walls at Amalienborg?

Amalienborg is many things: A home to the royal family, a royal headquarters and a workplace for employees of the court. The aim of this book is to offer a glimpse of the life behind the walls – and the Queen as well as Prince Henrik, the Crown Prince and the Crown Princess have agreed to talk about the palace, the monarchy and their work.

They each play a significant part in ensuring the unique commitment to the royal family. The cover of this book says it all: We see the royal family on the balcony, high above the palace square, and the Danes have turned up by the thousands to celebrate the monarch. With red and white flags flying, the picture could hardly be more Danish and it could be seen as emblematic of the people's unique support.

The skill, the wisdom and the sense of balance required to ensure the future of the monarchy is, however, not obvious to the naked eye. Many people would probably consider a royal family an anachronism in a modern society, but in Denmark the royal family has widespread public support.

In "Amalienborg", the reader will witness how the royal family and the court work to future-proof the monarchy and ensure that the institution remains rooted in the population.

While the powerful position of the monarchy has astonished even the Queen, she has also offered a possible explanation. In a globalized world, having something that ties nation and people together holds special value, something that – in the words of the Queen – enables you to say, "This is us".

An Architectural Gem

"When you stand at the Amalienborg Square, you find yourself inside a past idyll between the four beautiful Eigtved palaces that were not originally built as royal residencies, since the sovereigns of the day sought larger and more pompous conditions; yet one will have a hard time finding a grander and more stylish plaza. Name the monarch who lives better and more unassumingly? It is elegant in an open and friendly way, and all four palaces face the visitor, who, standing by the equestrian statue at the centre is among nothing but smiling facades. And so wonderfully has this complex been conceived that it completely excludes the outside world. Each palace welcomes the neighbouring mansion as its own mirror image, and no street perspective will lead the eye astray; the plaza is connected as a magic ring, and yet people from all four corners of the world arrive in a steady stream, as if from the wings of a theatre. No builder has constructed a more ideal stage for representation, at the same time open and yet closed on all sides. These palaces literally form a closed party. Amalienborg is the city's most festive and beautiful place, and the harmony here is perfect."

This is how, eighty-five years ago, the excellent but little known Copenhagen historian and topographer O.C. Nielsen summarized the history of Amalienborg. At that time, King Christian X was still relatively new in office, and in the years to come, a few more generations of the royal family have inhabited the magnificent palaces surrounding the square, and while the zeitgeist of the early twenty-first century is different in each and every sense of the word, the words remain in force: Amalienborg Palace is an architectural gem.

There is a unique harmony between the square with the equestrian statue in the centre and the four surrounding palaces. Add to this harmony the Marble Church as a point de vue, and the twin mansions of Dehn and Bernstorff, each occupying a corner of Frederiksgade and providing nothing less than a portal from Bredgade. Coupled with the mansions of Amaliegade and the immediate vicinity, these magnificent buildings constitute the basic elements of what unquestionably is the grandest district of the capital—the Frederiksstaden.

Nicolai Eigtved

Frederiksstaden and, especially, Amalienborg are primarily the result of one man's work, although obviously a number of other excellent artists and craftsmen were involved in the large-scale building project.

In 1701, Nicolai Eigtved was baptized Niels Madsen in the local parish church in Haraldsted on Central Zealand. His father, Mads Nielsen, was a poor copyholder of land at the Eigtwed farm, which was under the rule of the Skjoldenæsholm Estate. Once old enough, the boy Niels apprenticed here as a gardener. Fully trained he left for the capital and found employment at the Frederiksberg Garden, the country's largest park. At age 22, the journeyman gardener received a passport signed by King Frederik IV and went abroad to go on the tramp. The journey took him from Berlin to Warsaw, where he found work with the Saxon-Polish construction authorities who noticed that this man, with the title of captain, was an extremely talented manager in the construction of military fortifications.

It is not likely that he ever had any formal training in Den-

mark, but during his long stay abroad he learned to write German and apparently had no difficulties associating with the outstanding international architects who were hired by the many European Courts and princely houses. He absorbed knowledge greedily, no matter if the subject was ornamental gardening, construction of military facilities, urban planning, or church and castle building. And wherever he went, his drawings impressed people to such an extent that the King's Copenhagen began to take an interest in him. In 1732, a Danish diplomat in Berlin made sure Eigtved was appointed Danish Lieutenant and granted by the King the necessary funds for further studies in Italy, Austria and Bavaria. This took place during the years when French Rococo spread across the continent and in earnest caught on as the dominating style, having a significant influence on his development as an architect.

Twelve years had passed since journeyman gardener Niels Madsen had ventured into the world to perfect his skills, and now, in 1735, he returned as Nicolai Eigtved, celebrated royal builder and Captain of the Engineer Corps. At first he supervised the royal buildings of the provinces, but soon he became involved in the completion of the colossal Christiansborg Palace. He decorated the royal living quarters and made drawings for the Marble Bridge as well as two distinct pavilions that constituted a portal from the Frederiksholms Canal into the palace riding grounds. Eigtved also supplied the drawings for the Prince's Palace on the other side of the canal. The building had been built in 1743-44 to serve as housing for the country's Crown Prince, the later King Frederik V. In quick succession, Eigtved delivered the drawings for a number of mansions for the wealthy, as well as gazebos in both Northern and Southern Zealand. He was also entrusted with the task of erecting the first royal theatre on Kongens Nytorv (called the "Comedy House"), the King Frederik's Hospital (now Designmuseum Danmark), the Asiatic Company's warehouse and the Christian's Church in the district of Christianshavn. This was before the King commissioned him to realise the plans for the Frederiksstaden and Amalienborg.

The task was colossal, but Eigtved put his fingerprints everywhere, in matters large and small. The master town plan with Amaliegade as longitudinal axis and Frederiksgade as transverse axis was Eigtved's idea. The neighbourhood's newly constructed town houses and mansions were also built according to drawings that he had drafted and which, even before construction began, would be controlled by him, and this is what gives these streets their distinctive and harmonious character. Given that a high degree of variation is an essential feature of the Rococo, he didn't require the houses in the new district to be similar. Much was left to the builder's own desires and their economic standing, but he did insist on a few mandatory guidelines. The houses were to be of the same height, and cornices as well as windows had to be flush.

In his final year, Nicolai Eigtved became the first director of the newly established Academy of Art, but at his death in 1754, he had seen only the beginning of what would become his masterpiece. Moltke and Levetzau's palaces had been erected but an additional two had yet to be built. The same could be said for the church with its impressive dome, which he had drafted. He was buried in the herb garden of St. Petri Church. His sepulchral monument was destroyed in the bombardment of Copenhagen in 1807. For 150 years it was miss-

ing, but then, by chance, it popped up and presently hangs on the wall inside St. Peter's Church.

The Year of the Jubilee 1749

For the common Copenhagener—not to mention the country's farmers and residents of the market towns—1749 was most likely an ordinary year of drudgery and the few, meagre pleasures allotted to an honest, Christian man. But for the autocratic monarch, Frederik V and his immediate surroundings, 1749 was a jubilee to celebrate the 300 years that had passed since the Oldenburg dynasty had taken possession of the Danish throne. Strictly speaking, the anniversary should have been held one year earlier, as Count Diderik of Oldenburg in 1448 had been enthroned as Danish king under the name Christian I. That, however, had not been done, and there was no need to be too particular. One year more or less didn't matter in the bigger scheme of things.

The last days of October were devoted to the feast, and the preceding weeks had been spent on improving the condition of the capital as much as possible. Under normal circumstances, the air quality of mid-eighteenth century Copenhagen was not suited for delicate noses, and countless truckloads of household rubbish and animal as well as human droppings had exceptionally been shipped to the other side of the ramparts. Many residents had decorated their houses for the occasion, and all over the city, lights were placed on poles, fully illuminating the streets after nightfall. This was highly unusual since wintertime Copenhagen would normally be shrouded in complete darkness from early evening onward.

The Gammeltorv—or Old Square—where Copenhagen's first City Hall was located, was hardly recognisable. Here, the magistrate had erected a temple-like wooden building over the Caritas Fountain on the sides of which the spectator could study 300 years of royal portraits. One day saw celebration services in the Slotskirken Church, another offered speeches and lectures at the university, but the highpoint took place on the third day when the King laid the cornerstone to a new church, designed by the royal court architect Nicolai Eigtved and bearing the royal name of Frederik's Church. It was an imposing project, conceived as a tribute to the divine royal power, and a project, which ended up requiring more than one might have anticipated in terms of financial resources and patience.

No fewer than 145 years passed from the first sod to the dedication of the Marble Church in 1894. While preparing the first drawings for the church and its mighty dome, Eigtved already had the sketches ready for a entire new district to be built outside the old medieval town, in a part of New Copenhagen officially called Sankt Annæ Øster Kvarter (Saint Anne's Town), but which now and for more than 260 years has been called Frederiksstaden.

The royal affinity of the names of Frederik's Church and Frederiksstaden is by no means coincidental. The entire new district, at the outset the grandest in the capital, was erected in honour of the absolutist monarch who by his mercy held together the realms of Denmark and Norway, and who in his wisdom bestowed peace and prosperity on the people. Where the district's newly built streets intersected, Eigtved envisaged a formidable square with an equestrian statue of the noble King Frederik V as the absolute centre.

The nation did indeed experience an epoch of peace and prosperity for the next eighty years after the end of the Great Northern War in 1721. Trade flourished as never before, and Danish merchants and ship owners with their heavily laden ships brought home unbelievable sums of money back to the Danish seaports. In Copenhagen, the impact of wealth became visible in the new and magnificent mansions, the elegant town houses, and rows of spacious warehouses lining the streets along the quay.

It was also one of the nation's great merchants, Andreas Bjørn, who originally fostered the idea of settling the vast area along the coast between Sankt Annæ Gade and the Copenhagen customs house. He convinced some of the city's other big merchants to go along with the idea, but even before they began, the Lord High Steward Adam Gottlob Moltke caught a whiff of the building plans, and affairs took a completely new turn.

Throughout the summer months, the idea of building on the large, open area between Norgesgade (Bredgade) and the coast—and all the way out to the customs house—was presented to people who could influence the Central Administration. Here, the construction project was welcomed; the densely populated city had to develop where nature, as was the case here, presented the opportunities. People of imagination and insight agreed with Royal Builder Eigtved: Amalienborg Square was quite simply the best place in Copenhagen.

The initial plan was to build fine and sturdy citizen's houses, which of course would require the necessary building permits. The disaster of the Copenhagen Fire of 1728 was still fresh in memory, and the authorities sought to take all possible precautions. The Navy's presence in the waters off the coast was a particular problem, and the same applied to the timber dealers who had significant quantities of flammable wood stored on a crowded beach area along Toldbodgade. Since the Navy was not to be compromised on any account, a building permit issued by Holmen's commanding officer, Admiral Suhm, was required. The permit was given on the condition that the developers erected brick-build houses instead of the traditional half-timber houses, and that they made sure to keep fire hazardous occupations out of the neighbourhood. Space had to be found elsewhere in town for the manufacturing of beer, bread and schnapps.

The merchants' plans were presented to the King in early September, and then things began to move. Free of charge, Frederik V handed over the vast area of almost 600 by 270 meters to the City of Copenhagen, ordering them to prepare the site and find suitable builders who could meet the high demands associated with the royal gift.

Aside from the timber merchants, who had financial interests on the site and thus were first in line to choose lots, everyone, in principle, could sign up at City Hall for a free building site. Social status and civilian occupation could, however, not be entirely ignored.

The distribution of plots bear witness to this fact. The timber merchants and craftsmen mainly settled on either side of Amaliegade while the officials gathered in the somewhat finer Norgesgade. The subdivided plots varied in size but it was allowed to merge several of them, thus giving dignitaries an opportunity to build proper mansions with gardens.

The favourable conditions were supplemented even more

when the developers were granted a thirty-year lodging tax exemption, plus exemption from duty on building materials that had to be imported. The royal deed of gift did however come with certain requirements. If a plot after five years remained undeveloped, it was to be returned to the county, and to ensure that the new district in its entirety became an architectural whole, the developers were ordered to adhere to Court Architect Eigtved's directives regarding building height, position of windows and cornices (that were to be aligned) and the general appearance of the facades on the street. This prestigious neighbourhood—so it was stated—must be characterized by the highest degree of evenness and regularity.

At a furious pace, Eigtved drew up a plan for the entire area, including the locations of Amaliegade and Frederiksgade, as well as the central square where they intersect. In addition to facade drawings for townhouses, he drafted the four identical palaces surrounding the square. The whole thing was over in a few weeks and the plan seemed perfect. They even found a plot with the right location for the district's new church, right across Norgesgade (Bredgade). Since the plot was a garden owned by the King's aunt, the acquisition caused no problems. All of this took place in the weeks leading up to the great anniversary festival to celebrate the Court by founding a new district, a prestigious building project unparalleled in the history of the capital, with the exception of the colossal Christiansborg Palace and its riding grounds which had been completed a few years earlier, and where Eigtved had also played a crucial role.

At this point, Adam Gottlob Moltke was already engaged in the project. Bearing the title of Lord High Steward, he was the King's closest advisor. Though formally without political influence for the better part of his life, he remained the kingdom's most powerful man and in the years to come he became the decisive driving force behind the plan.

It was the wish of Frederik V to retain the right to dispose of the four palace plots surrounding the central square, so it was most likely not a coincidence that Moltke became the first to choose. The plot in the southwest corner was the most attractive. The soil here was not quite as swampy as closer to the coast, and the garden behind the building would be perfectly situated relative to the sun.

An official deed was drafted, and no later than the following year, Moltke would embark on the complex excavations. A lot of digging was needed, and that was a job suitable for soldiers. In order to divert surface water, the dirt was thrown into the canal encircling the area. The pumps ran incessantly to keep the excavation nothing but reasonably dry, and more than 700 solid posts for the pile foundation were driven into the ground before the bricklayers commenced on the actual construction.

By August, the developer could lay down the corner stone of his mansion, and on a copper plate, discovered in 1977, he solemnly expressed his undying gratitude to the noble king— 'Friderich the fifth'—and his grace and good deeds. Though the German-born and German-speaking Moltke had tremendous influence on the political decision-making process of the mid-eighteenth century, he knew his place in the absolutist Danish monarchy. In 1743, serving as Lord Chamberlain for Crown Prince Frederik, it had been his duty to watch over the prince's moral character—a highly demanding task. Moltke

became a father figure of a sort to the young man, and three years later, when the prince became king, Moltke was promoted Lord High Steward and became the King's closest advisor.

It is well known that Frederik V as a consequence of his dissipated life often was unable to assume the duties of an absolute monarch, and it was on this basis that Moltke in reality became the most important political force of the kingdom. As early as 1751, the Lord High Steward held the ceremony of raising the rooftree, and only three years later he invited the monarch and the dignitaries of the country for supper in his new house. This took place on Saturday March 30, 1754. One can only assume that everyone must have been taken aback by the unimaginable treasures of the artistic decorations, outside as well as inside, and the extreme wealth of the developer now became evident. His work at the Court cleared the way for him to fill the post as Præses (Candidate, i.e. Chief Executive) of the kingdom's most important trading company, the Asian Company.

Later in the day, when the distinguished gentlemen and their wives finished eating and drinking, they, as was the custom, went on to the Charlottenborg Palace, where the King in person visited the Art Academy along with the Præses and manager of the institution. It was an intimate group of people he already knew and had confidence in—a group consisting of only Adam Gottlob Moltke and Nicolai Eigtved.

Sophie Amalienborg

As mentioned, the four palaces that make up Amalienborg had been constructed in the 1750s according to an overall

plan. But the story of Amalienborg begins 100 years earlier somewhere else in town. On the other side of Vesterport, approximately at the present location of Copenhagen Central Station, the wife of Frederik III, Queen Sophie Amalie, had a pleasure garden. The garden had been maltreated by Swedish troops during the siege of Copenhagen in 1658-59, and when peace once again descended on town and country, she began the search for a safer location inside the ramparts.

Her father-in-law, Christian IV, had taken steps to double the area of Copenhagen by moving the city gate and the capital's ramparts to the north, from Kongens Nytorv and Gothersgade to the current location at Østerport. Rosenborg Palace and its appurtenant gardens thus came to be located in the New Copenhagen, as the district soon would be called. In contrast to the densely populated medieval town, New Copenhagen had plenty of room and open spaces, and it wasn't easy to motivate people to move that far away from their familiar surroundings. It therefore seemed natural for Sophie Amalie to establish the Queen's Garden as a companion to the King's Garden in this rural environment. She acquired the entire area between the current Sankt Annæ Plads and Fredericiagade, an area stretching from the coast to Bredgade. Granted, in was unpleasant to walk about in this swampy morass, but something could be done about that. In 1664, the Municipal Authority were given the orders to use the capital's considerable quantities of street refuse as landfill in the beach meadow, and a few years later, Toldbodgade was built on a dike along the coast. The Queen was quite evidently fond of her garden, and when Frederik III died in 1670 she built in the garden a summer palace that would serve as her dower

house. It was a three-story building with a central dome, and it was aptly named Sophie Amalienborg. In the last decade of her life she enjoyed the summer palace and its sprawling garden, and after her death, Christian V took possession of the property. Sophie Amalienborg was well suited for festive gatherings, which was the reason why the King, on April 15, 1689, celebrated his 44th birthday out here, at a distance from the old royal palace of Christiansborg. The celebration included a gala performance in a theatre building that was connected to one of the summer palace's side pavilions by a Colonnade.

The gala performance and the opera, "The Vereinigte Göttersteit" was attended by the city's most prominent people and turned out to such an overwhelming success that it was restaged four days later for the lower social classes. Children and adults alike rejoiced at the prospect of experiencing something new and exciting. None of them had previously seen an opera—all that music and song, all those candles and fireworks—and the auditorium was crammed to the rafters with two hundred people attending. The prologue went well, but before the real show had even begun, a wick from one of a thousand oil lamps fell into some dry juniper twigs. Seconds later, the thin silk fabric hanging on the walls—oil-soaked for extra effect—had caught fire. Panic set in and everyone went for the only door in the auditorium. The door, however, opened inward, and pressure from the terror-stricken crowd made it impossible to open.

Due to safety considerations, the windows of the auditorium had been barred, making escape equally impossible. In fifteen minutes, the makeshift wooden hut became a glowing heap of ashes in which almost all of the two hundred people perished. In addition, the palace itself caught fire and could not be saved. The materials that could be salvaged were reused in the construction of the Garrison Church at the end of the Dronningens Have. Thus the Sophie Amalienborg disappeared, but the name lived on. At his enthronement in 1670, Christian V had already made plans to replace Copenhagen Castle with a modern residence that reflected the ostentatious needs of the absolute monarchy. In the 1690s, Sweden's great architect Nicodemus Tessin was encouraged to prepare drawings for a project not unlike the vast royal palace he had mastered in Stockholm. The first sketches must have been to the King's liking, for he went ahead and had Tessin build a model—six meters long and one and a half meters tall—of the future palace to be erected in the Amalienborg Have. A designated ship ferried the model to Copenhagen where it was displayed in a building that had been built for the occasion at the very spot where Frederikskirken was to be built. That was how far the magnificent project went. Economic difficulties were piling up, and relations with Sweden had impaired to the extent where any cooperation was precluded. Christian V died in 1699, and one year later, the two Nordic countries were on a war footing.

For more than a dozen years, the site of the fire lay waste and desolate. When finally the last vestiges of the summer palace had been cleared away, the part of the site closest to Sankt Annæ Plads was designated as royal pleasure garden, and the part closest to the Citadel was zoned for a roll-call square for the Copenhagen garrison. Where the garden and the square met, an octagonal pavilion was erected to accommodate the King when he inspected his troops. At this time, the entire area of the garden and drill grounds were enclosed by canals on all four sides, and avenues of lime trees were planted along the Sankt Annæ Plads and Bredgade. In 1728, the capital saw its first devastating town fire, and though the reconstructions required tremendous efforts, Christian VI began in the 1730s to demolish the old palace on the Slotsholmen Island in order to build a new royal palace.

As was customary, the palace bore the developer's name and swallowed up more than three-quarters of the state budget, but in return the nation was given a royal residence of a splendour and embellishment unequalled anywhere in Northern Europe. For years to come, no one took any interest in the area surrounding the Amalienborg Palace, until the King in 1743 asked Nicolai Eigtved to prepare drawings for a new palace for the Crown Prince. It was to be situated on the Frederiksholms Channel, straight across from Christiansborg riding grounds. Boldly, Eigtved proposed to the King and Lord Chamberlain Moltke another location for the prince's palace—"as the Amalienborg Square is surely considered the best in Copenhagen." But Christian V did not agree, and thus Eigtved built the Marble Bridge and the Prince's Palace, which today houses the National Museum at Frederiksholms Channel. The architect had however succeeded in directing the monarch's attention to the almost forgotten area at the other end of town, an area that had been named after the King's great-grandmother and where she had at one time had a summer palace.

Moltke - And all the others

By the time Frederik V handed over the building lots to the City of Copenhagen—while reserving the right to dispose of the Amalienborg square—it was already clear that four identical palaces would be erected according to Eigtved's drawings, and that the King's confidant, Lord High Steward A.G. Moltke, would get to pick first. The identity of the other developers was not revealed until early May 1750. The deed to the plot next to Moltke's, on the northwest side of the square, was transferred to Lieutenant General Count C.F. Raben Levetzau. On the southeast side, Privy Councillor Baron Joachim Brockdorff was chosen to build a mansion. Finally, advisor to the King, Severin Løvenskiold (with the obsolete title of Konferensråd) became the fourth and last noblemen to be found worthy of the task.

For Moltke, Levetzau and Brockdorff, the building activity would not give rise to economic problems, and they immediately devoted themselves to the task. For the young Løvenskiold, however, the situation was different. More than a year passed before he got started. Even with the privileges promised by the King, the distinguished and expensive building had burdened the economy of the Privy. As the house took shape, the problems grew larger, and in 1754, he had to hand the unfinished palace over to the immensely rich Dowager Countess Anne Sophie Schack. Not that she wanted to live there; she had recently purchased Admiral Niels Juel's large mansion on the corner of Kongens Nytorv and Bredgade. But her grandson, Count Hans Schack was about to be married—with the daughter of neighbour A.G. Moltke, to boot—and a palace at the Amalienborg Square was considered a suitable first step for the young couple.

As it turned out, they didn't stay long. A few years later, Count Schack was appointed prefect of his native part of the country and moved to Møgeltønder where he owned the Schackenborg Palace. He would, however, also run into financial problems and was put under the administration of the treasury. As part of the solution, Schack's Palace was subleased to people who could appreciate living well and who were undeterred by the rent at the city's most expensive address.

Following the general's death in 1756, a similar thing happened at Levetzau's Palace. Baron Brockdorff owned several estates in Schleswig where he preferred to stay, and even before his death in 1763 he had found suitable tenants for his Amalienborg Palace. It was three young princes of Hessen-Kassel. Two of them later established families with Danish princesses. When Moltke bought Brockdorff's possessions in southern Jutland to give them to one of his sons, the palace at Amalienborg was part of the deal. Moltke, however, sold it on to Frederik V, and that's how the King, shortly before his death in 1766, became the owner of one of the palaces that he 15 years earlier had ordered to be built.

While in the possession of the royal family, the palace was converted to an Academy for Army and Navy cadets, although the responsible architect found it to be obvious that "no building could be less suited as an institution for cadets." The architect's word, however, had no importance, and in the years until 1827, cavalry, infantry and navy officers were trained in Brockdorff's magnificent rococo building.

THE EQUESTRIAN STATUE

Even the very first sketches presented to the King in the early autumn of 1749 had the outline of a monument in the middle of the square between the four palaces. So the idea wasn't new when the German professor at the Art Academy, Marcus Tuscher, the following year drew up a project for an equestrian statue in a heavy baroque style with an abundance of allegorical figures in a water basin around a high pedestal. That, however, was a far as they came, as Tuscher died a few months later. It was out of the question that any Danish artist could properly perform the work, and the foreign minister, J.H.E. Bernstorff, gave the first secretary of legation in Paris the orders to find the right man. At this time, the famous Edme Bouchardon was in the process of creating an equestrian statue of Louis XV to be erected on the Place Royale, so he declined, but did recommend the young and talented Jacques François Joseph Saly from Valenciennes. Saly accepted the conditions, which promised him a fee of 35.000 rix-dollars, plus a well-paid professorship and free residence at Charlottenborg. He arrived in 1753, half a year late, and since the plan called for him to be away from home for five years, he had brought along to Copenhagen his parents and two unmarried sisters.

In his capacity of Præses, or Chief Executive, of Asiatic Company, Moltke made the voluminous cash pile of the Company available to cover the running costs. This, as things turned out, was a bold disposition. A year and a half later, Saly was ready to show sketches of how he imagined the equestrian statue, and how the pedestal was envisioned as a work of art unto itself. On the long sides he had placed two allegorical bronze figures, symbolizing Denmark and Norway. From two additional figures, symbolizing the Baltic and the North Sea, water poured into a basin that encircled the entire monument.

It was done in the style of the modern neoclassicism that had been such a success for Bouchardon in Paris. Saly considered for quite some time how to make the King. A certain degree of likeness was needed, but at the same time the commissioned work called for a glorification of the absolute monarchy as a concept. This is the basis on which one should contemplate the equestrian statue of Frederik V in the guise of the Roman imperator.

Selecting Saly for this task was bold indeed. He had previously made an equestrian statue and spent more than a year in the royal stables making drawings of horses seen from all sides. Twelve selected Frederiksborgers (Denmark's oldest horse breed) were put at his disposal, and it wasn't until he had finished this process that he began to model an actual model of a horse and rider in 1/6 scale. That part of the work took another year. At least a dozen plaster casts were made from the model, some of them sold through the Adresseavisen newspaper. The price was 20 rix-dollars, and the horse alone could be acquired for half that amount. This took place late in 1758, at a time when the job, according to his contract, should have been finished already. That was not the case, far from it, and another five years passed before a full-scale plaster model could be seen in a special studio in the garden of Charlottenborg.

In the meantime, search had begun for a bronze caster to assume the task. A Swede, Gerhard Meyer, had been considered but was discarded after making a bust of the King. A Frenchman, Pierre Gor, had cast the statue of Louis XV in Paris and he became the one to undertake the task of perpetuating Saly's work of art in bronze. He and his colleagues arrived in Denmark in 1764, where they moved into the old cannon foundry, Gjethuset. It was located at Kongens Nytorv, near Charlottenborg, on the site where more than 10 years later the Royal Theatre was built. The cannon production was moved to Generalkrigskommissær (the officer in charge of national conscription) J.F. Classen's factory in Frederiksværk—and that's how year after year went with preparations.

The casting itself would take only a few minutes, but transforming the plaster model to a complete work of art in bronze was an incredibly complicated process. March 2, 1764 was the crucial day toward which everyone anxiously looked: The day in which the liquid bronze would be poured into the mould. It was successful, although Saly

wasn't quite satisfied with the work performed by Gor and his assistants. Supposedly, a scuffle broke out between the two distinguished Frenchmen.

After a few months of finishing, the more than 22-ton equestrian statue was ready to be transported to Amalienborg. This task was left to court carpenter Joseph Zuber, who also worked as chief engineer at the Hofteatret (Court Theatre). He constructed an ingenious mechanism with hoists and pulleys, enabling half a hundred strong sailors to lift the colossus up on a sledge. Other soldiers were deployed to deliver the traction power when, during a few days in mid-August, the sledge on tracks covered the distance from the Kongens Nytorv to its destination at the Amalienborg Square. Moltke and the directors of Asiatic Company witnessed the scene, and the solemnity of the new equestrian statue of Frederik V passing the eighty year old statue of Christian V on horseback at the centre of Kongens Nytorv was marked by a twenty-seven shot gun salute from the Company's ships.

Frederiksgade, where the sledge

was to be reversed in order for horse and rider to be pulled backwards toward the pedestal on the square, was reached late in the afternoon. The reversing took place the following day, on August 16. The monument was lifted into place, and the heavy iron bars protruding from the pedestal up through three of the horse's legs to hold the equipage in place turned out to be a perfect fit. Yet again, a salute came from the ships in the harbour. On this occasion, no less than three times twenty-seven shots.

15 years had passed since the idea of the equestrian statue had been conceived in 1749, but work on the most expensive work of art in the history of Denmark was far from over. Four years earlier, Moltke, who had a weakness for historical dates, had laid down the cornerstone of the pedestal. This happened on October 18, the 100th anniversary of the introduction of the absolute monarchy in 1660. The unstable subsoil had necessitated substantial piling, but once completed, Saly could begin building the pedestal that some day would carry horse and rider, but which should also appear as a unique

work of art unto itself. This required large quantities of Italian marble and other precious materials, so expenses grew and soon money was no longer in abundance. Though the Asiatic Company was the nation's largest trading company, the cash box was not bottomless.

Due to the financial curtailment, Saly had to alter the ornamentation—and thus Denmark, Norway and the characters symbolizing the surrounding waters as well as some other ornaments was retrenched. In place, Saly drew four more modest tablets with an inscription in Latin telling of the King's great achievements as protector of the arts, science, industry and commerce.

The Company, however, would not be paying for the railing encircling the statue. It was forged at the expense of Generalkrigskommissær Classen at the industrial establishment in Frederiksværk. And it was no insignificant gift. The price was 10.000 rix-dollars, an amount equal to the price of a town house in Bredgade.

Paving the square was the only thing that needed to be done before the unveiling of the finished work

could finally take place. It happened in late October 1774. By this time, Christian VII had replaced Frederik V on the throne, and Count Moltke lived a quiet life on the Bregentved Estate, far away from the influence he once had. A few months earlier, Saly had returned home to France, peeved and bitter, as he felt deprived of the agreed-upon fee. Now it was time for the books to be balanced. Twenty years had passed and the equestrian statue had cost close to 550.000 rix-dollars. That was fifteen times as much as Saly's original contract, and more than the total expenses of building the entire Amalienborg a dozen years earlier. It was a staggering amount of money that for a long time would trouble the shareholders of Asiatic Company, but in return a unique piece of art had been made available for the nation to contemplate and admire.

The Royal Family Becomes Homeless

Late in the afternoon on February 26, 1794, fifteen-year old Adam Oehlenschläger observed from Frederiksberg how a red glow above Copenhagen gained momentum and gradually illuminated all of the dark winter sky. A few hours earlier, one of the court servants had discovered that a fire had broken out at Christiansborg. This, unfortunately, was discovered far too late. The fire already had a firm grip and quickly spread from room to room of the largest and costliest palace in Northern Europe. The next day, sooty remains of stonework jutted up through heaps of ashes. The first Christiansborg Palace with its magnificent furnishings and an abundance of valuable works of art had stood only half a century. It was a national disaster. The royal family, who each winter resided at the palace, had been evacuated in time and brought to safety, but with the fire, King Christian VII and the de facto reigning Crown Prince Frederik had been rendered homeless.

General von Huth in the Gjethuset on Kongens Nytorv accommodated father and son the first night, but a cannon foundry was not a suitable place for state business. For that reason, the King and Crown Prince moved in with foreign minister A.P. Bernstorff, who lived in the mansion at the corner of Bredgade (Norgesgade) and Frederiksgade, while the rest of the royal family were quartered at the Rosenborg, Sorgenfri and Fredensborg palaces.

The very same foreign minister had been selected as executor of Moltke's estate, who had died a year and a half earlier, making it unproblematic even in the following days to negotiate the King's purchase of the palace at Amalienborg. The building was unoccupied but still fur-nished and virtually unaltered after the late Count and Lord High Steward. The purchase contract was signed on the third day after the fire, and the price was extraordinarily reasonable. The amount, 45.000 rix-dollars, was 20,000 rix-dollars under the appraisal by the fire insurance. To obtain adequate housing for the Crown Prince, Schack's Palace on the other side of Amaliegade was bought a few days later. It was considerably cheaper, as this palace needed a thorough restoration before it could be used, and a long line of tenants had not treated the delicate interior gently. Finally, the Heir Presumptive—the King's half-brother—bought Levetzau's Palace across Frederiksgade for 30.000 rix-dollars.

The royal family had made its entrance at Amalienborg, and the entire operation had taken nothing but a few days. Although the fire at Christiansborg had been absolutely devastating, some furniture had been salvaged from the burning building, and the most valuable items came to use in the new homes of the King and Crown Prince. A throne with a canopy was brought down from Frederiksborg Palace to what was now called "The King's Palace", and a new billiards table was set up so the monarch could keep up his interest in this noble game.

Given that Schack's Palace was in no useable condition at first, the King was accommodated at Moltke's palace along with the Crown Prince and his wife and child. The King resided on the first floor, called the beletagen, and the Crown Prince couple had the ground floor—the Crown Prince in the north part and the Crown Princess in the south part of the palace, as was customary. Room was

found on the mezzanine and in the basement for servants and the necessary entourage.

Compared with the enormous Christiansborg Palace, room was scarce at Amalienborg for nobility as well as servants, and in early May the whole family travelled to the summer residence at the spacious Frederiksberg Palace. This happened a few weeks earlier than normal, if not more, but it was important for the craftsmen to commence their work; there was much to be achieved, and time was short.

The Colonnade

The responsibility for the rebuilding and the extensive repair work was put into the hands of the professor of architecture at the Art Academy, Royal Architect Caspar Frederik Harsdorff. He soon had the first drafts ready, and when financing was in place, a royal decree resolved that work could begin. That summer, with the nobility residing on the countryside, Harsdorff was busier than ever. And it didn't help that half of the Copenhagen carpenters along with other craftsmen had decided to go on a strike, making it necessary to summon for a short period the assistance of the Holmen shipwrights. The two hundred carpenters who had gone on strike were placed in the spacious dungeons of the Citadel, where they were offered

---

A valet in the antechamber of the military colours at Christian IX's Palace.

the choice of labouring in shackles or to continue with paid employment.

The low gatehouses that had connected the four palaces with the associated pavilions at the street corners were raised by one storey. While this ruined Eigtved's beautiful marble terraces, it did create interior space for the many necessary activities without significantly blemishing the overall, elegant architectural impression. Nonetheless, Harsdorff's greatest architectural achievement in connection with the reconstruction was his ingenious solution to the problem of establishing a direct connection between the palaces of the King and Crown Prince, a connection necessitated by certain prevailing conditions in the family. Christian VII suffered from a mental illness that made it impossible for him to perform his royal duties. Thus it was the Crown Prince, the later King Frederik VI who performed the father's tasks as regent. The throne room was located in the King's palace, which also housed the Council of State and the large evening parties, so quite a bit of traffic between the two buildings was to be expected. Driving back and forth in a coach would be impractical, and no one dared to even think that people of such descent would walk under the open sky.

That spring, Harsdorff had the drawings ready for a new characteristic edifice. The Colonnade with its eight Ionic pillars in Neoclassical style was erected as soon as the drawings had been approved. It constituted a gateway between Amaliegade and the Amalienborg Square, and conjoined, in astonishing harmony, with Eigtved's rococo architecture. A two and a half meters wide corridor with

natural light and a ceiling height of about two meters was established under the roof facing the square; behind the corridor were three spacious rooms, and this solved the problem of the missing link between the two buildings. It was simple and at the same time constructive, and it's difficult nowadays to even imagine Amalienborg without the Colonnade.

The Colonnade was in place even before the royal family returned from their summer residence in the Frederiksberg district. The assignment had been put out to tender and conditions had been clear from the beginning. The work had to be done in a hurry and the materials had to be more or less the cheapest available. The King's sojourn at Amalienborg was seen as nothing but a temporary solution to the housing problem. Once the Christiansborg Palace had been reconstructed, the Colonnade would no longer serve any purpose, and that's why wood was chosen as the material for the columns. It was much cheaper than sandstone, and even wooden columns could be expected to last at least a dozen years. They were painted in an appropriate shade of gray, and when the workmen tossed sea sand on the still wet paint, no one could tell that it wasn't the real thing. The budget as well as the tight schedule had been met, and everything had been rectified when, later in the year, the King and Crown Prince returned each to their palace in the capital.

Gala and battalion colours no longer in use are kept at the residential palace.

The Amalienborg of the Kings

Rebuilding the ruined Christiansborg Palace dragged on. The task in itself was enormous, but the problems increased manifold in the following year, when Copenhagen was hit by a town fire of almost the same magnitude as the one in 1728, which had laid close to a third of the capital in ashes.

A large part of the many homeless families were accommodated in the sooty palace ruins, where they stayed for years, and then it was as if the accidents knew no end. An unfortunate policy pulled Denmark into the Napoleonic Wars. And there seemed to be insufficient strength and economy to realize C.F. Hansen's plan from 1800 to rebuild the palace as royal residence. In 1807, Copenhagen was struck by the first terrorist city bombing in the history of war, and the subsequent seven-year war with England led to the state bankruptcy of 1813, and the painful loss of Norway the following year. Not until 1828 had work on the neoclassical palace come to a point where it could accommodate the royal family. By now, however, it was no longer relevant.

Christian VII stayed in Moltke's Palace until his death in 1808. At this time, the palace officially bore the King's name, and subsequently the rooms were turned into offices for the many public servants of the Court. Frederik VI who for years, even as Crown Prince, had been the de facto regent of the kingdom decided to stay in Schack's Palace, where he had moved after the palace fire in 1794.

For a dozen of years, Christian VII's Palace served as headquarters for the Ministry of Foreign Affairs, and in 1865 it was converted into banquet and reception rooms for King Christian IX. And as the children of Christian IX and Queen Louise married into the royal houses of Sweden, England, Greece, and Russia, the royal family needed more space suitable for official state visits and private family gatherings.

Christian VII's Palace was always the most richly ornamented of the four palaces, and with a thorough modernisation of interior and exterior from 1982 to 1996 it's also the best preserved. For more than two hundred years the building has, however, not accommodated a regent and is used exclusively for entertainment purposes. The banqueting hall—usually agreed by experts to have nation's most exclusive Rococo interior—is only put to ceremonial use, such as the traditional New Year's banquet and in connection with state visits, where the newly refurbished rooms and bedrooms can be used to accommodate guests.

Following the death of Frederik VI in 1839, Dowager Queen Marie Sophie Frederikke resided in Schack's Palace for a dozen more years. It later served as the seat of the Supreme Court, and in 1865, after the necessary renovations, it became the residence of King Christian IX and his queen. Christian IX died in 1906, but the King's name remains associated with this palace, which since 1972 has been the residence of Queen Margrethe II.

The cleaning of Amalienborg is one of the Matron of the Household's responsibilities. It's hard work for the cleaning ladies because of the many square feet.

Brockdorff's Palace was the only Palace to be acquired as royal property even before the fire of 1794 had made the royal family homeless. In 1768, the building was converted into a military academy, first for Army cadets, and after 1788 for Navy cadets. The Banquet Hall was turned into a gymnasium, and the building suffered much wear and tear inside and outside. A major overhaul was therefore needed before Crown Prince Frederik, the later King Frederik VII, in 1828 could move in with his consort, Vilhelmine Marie. The marriage did not last, and King Frederik VI deported the prince, who lived a rather debauched life in the capital, to Fredericia. The Crown Prince was later appointed governor of the Island of Funen. When he became king in 1848, he chose to reside at Christiansborg Palace, where he also had an apartment fitted out for his morganatic wife, Louise Rasmussen, who after the wedding ceremony in 1850 was elevated to Countess of Danner. This makes Frederik VII the only monarch since the ill-fated palace fire not to reside at Amalienborg.

The very year after he became king, Frederik VII signed the Constitution that marked the final end of the absolute monarchy. This meant that Amalienborg became state property and that the palaces not inhabited by the King would in the future be made available for practical purpos-

The Banquet Hall in Christian IX's Palace, from where the Royal Family steps out on the balcony.

es, such as a public museum or domicile for a ministry. The Dowager Queen after Christian VIII lived in Levetzau's Palace, and the widow of Frederik VI in Schack's Palace. Nobody had the heart to remove the two senescent ladies from their homes and it was decided to let the royals stay for life. With the death of Dowager Queen Marie Sophie Frederikke in 1852, some of the critical space problems were solved: The Supreme Court was awarded the bele-tage with the prestigious banquet hall in Schack's Palace, and a few years later the Ministry of Foreign Affairs moved into the ground floor.

In 1869, Crown Prince Frederik, the later King Frederik VIII moved into Brockdorff's Palace with his wife, Princess Louise, and they lived there for years, until he in 1906 succeeded his father on the throne. Frederik VIII has given his name to the palace, which in 1935 was adapted for another Crown Prince Frederik, later King Frederik IX and Queen Ingrid, and this is where their three daughters, Margrethe, Benedikte and Anne-Marie grew up. The building has recently been completely restored, and the palace named after King Frederik VIII of Denmark will become Denmark's next royal residence when Crown Prince Frederik one day succeeds his mother, becoming the tenth Frederik in a row.

The palace fire of 1794 affected the whole royal family, including Christian VII's eight years younger half brother, Frederik, bearing the title Heir Presumptive. He acquired Levetzau's Palace, which the owner, Privy Councillor Levetzau had long tried unsuccessfully to divest. Here the presumptive heir to the throne lived with his wife, Sophie

Frederikke of Mecklenburg-Schwerin, and after his death in 1805 the palace was taken over by their son, Christian Frederik, the later King Christian VIII. He gave the palace its royal name, and this was the home in which the well-read and intelligent King brought together a large number of the authors, artists and scientists of the Golden Age.

After the King's death in 1848, Dowager Queen Caroline Amalie stayed at Christian VIII's Palace for another thirty-three years. She died in 1881, and when the second Christiansborg Palace burned down three years later, the palace for some years served as the seat of the Ministry of Foreign Affairs. In 1898, Prince Christian, the later Christian X, married the Grand Duchess Alexandrine of Mecklenburg-Schwerin, and on this occasion the couple moved into Christian VIII's Palace, which thus became the residence during King Christian X's thirty-five year long reign.

In 1918, when the two houses of Denmark's bicameral parliament, the Folketing and the Landsting moved back to the present Christiansborg Palace on the castle island, a lot indicated that Christian X would also move into the royal residence of the newly built palace. That, however, never came to pass. After some deliberation, the royal family chose to stay at Amalienborg.

Preparing the New Year's Banquet at Christian VII's Palace.

KING, KING, DO COME OUT

"Thousands and thousands of people filled the Amalienborg Square, bringing traffic to a standstill in the nearby streets."

For the past 100 years, and with very little variation in the choice of words, this is how the newspapers of Denmark usually describe royal birthdays and other festive events in the royal family. Even the spectacle that ensued on the Queen's 70th birthday has not yet been forgotten. Nonetheless, the palace square has on three occasions in the twentieth century set the scene for large popular gatherings that can rightfully be described as political manifestations of a historical nature. These took place despite the fact that the country's head of state has no authority to partake in the political decision-making process.

This has, from time to time, been put forward as the principal reason for locating the monarch's residence at the Amalienborg Palace and the political leadership of the country, the government and the Folketing, at Slot-sholmen. This is also the reason why the Christiansborg Palace Square became the obvious place for citizens to gather and vent their displeasure. The equestrian statue of Frederik VII—the very King who gave the country its constitution—is constantly the centre of large and small demonstrations. These demonstrations are generally directed against the incumbent government, as is the custom in a country with right of assembly and freedom of speech. By contrast, it's exceedingly rare to have political demonstrations at the Amalienborg Palace. Nonetheless, the twentieth century saw this happen on three occasions, which were or could have become epoch-making. Each time the protagonist was King Christian X.

The Women's Procession of 1915

In 1915, a review of the Constitution, including a reform of the electoral law passed with no significant opposition through both bicameral chambers—the Folketing and the Landsting. This granted women and servants the right to vote to the country's legislative assembly, while people with no wealth could now vote in elections to the Landsting. As was required, the King signed the law at the Council of State on 5 June. But he did a poor job hiding his reluctance to the new constitution and its effects. However, all four parties agreed politically and he was left no choice. The thing that perhaps annoyed him most was that the head of government henceforth (as in the other Nordic countries) would be called Prime Minister instead of President of the Council. This was deliberate manifestation of the fact that the ministers from now on were to be perceived as servants of the State, not as members of the King's council.

It was a celebration nonetheless, and the King had to come to terms with it. The solemn formalities were taken care of at the meeting in the residential palace between the monarch and the convened government. The King placed his monogram on the new constitution while on the square outside a procession of white-clad women arrived to express their gratitude. Naturally, everything was

prearranged, and the organizers took it for granted that the King would be happy to receive the delegation of women who had come to thank him for the franchise.

But he was deeply opposed to the procession. It was not according to his wish that the electoral law had been expanded to include the female part of the population. Pressed hard, he met with the delegation, where he in a few words expressed that women, in his view, belonged in the home: "Here, the influence of women cannot be replaced, for it is by way of the child's love for the home that the love for our mutual home, Denmark, is awakened."

Among the attending women was Commander Emma Gad, who later became famous in another context entirely. She had the opportunity to express her feelings in a conversation with the King: "Your Majesty! This is the happiest day of my life," to which the King allegedly replied: "Quite, but I do believe you should rather go home and make coffee for your husband." Christian X was not a women's right advocate.

The Easter Crisis of 1920

On the Monday following Palm Sunday, 1920, the country's Social-Liberal Prime Minister Carl Th. Zahle had been called in audience at the King's residence. It was no secret that the personal relationship between the two men was anything but cordial, and politically there was hardly any point on which they agreed. Zahle had been prime minister since 1913, and the King had long wanted a new government as he fervently opposed a number of the incumbent government's most significant actions. This included the Constitution of 1915 and the already made decision to sell the Danish West Indian Islands the following year, but the crucial antagonism between the Social-Liberal government and the King became evident in connection with the reunification of Southern Jutland with Denmark. The public was strongly divided on where to draw the new border between Denmark and Germany, and the conservative parties demanded the issue resolved by an election.

The King supported this view, but the parliamentary majority consisting of Social-Liberals and Social Democrats were reluctant to meet the requirement until after a new electoral law had been passed. This was the situation that fateful Monday, March 29, when the prime minister met with the King at Amalienborg. It's unlikely that Christian X had decided in advance to dismiss the prime minister, but given how the conversation developed, this became the consequence. The King told Zahle in no uncertain terms that he wanted an early election. This was refused. When he asked if the government would resign, Zahle said that he could not justify such an action, given the parliamentary majority, but that "the King is at liberty to dismiss the ministry."

That comment triggered the drama. Zahle was dismissed and thanked for the years the collaboration had lasted—and from one moment to the next, the country had plunged into the most perilous domestic situation in recent times. During the course of that evening, a clash between police and angry protesters evolved in the neighbourhood of Amalienborg. The Co-penhagen Police Department had deployed eighty men to cover the square, and later in the evening they were supplemented by one hundred and twenty guardsmen, who would take action only if absolutely necessary.

Combating the riots was seen as a police mission, and military intervention could too easily make it seem that the revolution had broken out in the nation. The following days saw further popular meetings around the city. The Syndicalists gathered on the Fælleden commons under the slogan, "Down with the monarchy", but aside from that, the city was fairly quiet on Maundy Thursday and Good Friday. A delegation from Copenhagen City Council had requested a meeting with the King at Amalienborg on Easter Eve. It could be seen as a first step toward the revolution, just as when the Communards seized power during the Paris Commune. For fear that it in any case would bring the situation out of control, the ordinary guard at Amalienborg was augmented and the Copenhagen garrison put on alert.

Though the police had barricaded

the entire area, it was impossible to hold back the crowd. The atmosphere was more than incited, and the accounts of just how many people forced their way to the Palace Square differ significantly. The police said 10.000. The Syndicalist newspaper—Solidarity—estimated the figure to be 100.000. Others believed that the crowd had not exceeded the number of people who usually turn up on Sundays to watch the changing of the guard.

At one point, shots were fired near the equestrian statue, but what really happened has never been explained. Then the protesters took to the streets where the excitement evolved into vandalism. The calm did not come, and around midnight about 4.000 people once again forced their way toward Amalienborg, where the guard yet again had been augmented, and violent street battles ensued around the Frederiksstaden district. This continued the following days and nights. Amalienborg was assailed by syndicalists and left-wing socialists demanding the abolition of the monarchy.

The air was thick with revolution and the constitutional monarchy had never been in a more threatened position. The danger passed, however, over the course of the week after the excited Easter days. The Social Democrats led by Thorvald Stauning eventually managed to curb the tempers; the great Labour Party saw no political interest in a continued unrest that could not be controlled by the freely elected leadership of the labour movement.

The Farmer's Procession (Bondetoget) 1935

It was common knowledge in 1935 that Mussolini had come to power in Italy after the March on Rome, thirteen years earlier. Since then, the ideas of fascism had spread beyond the European continent and thrived in Denmark mainly in certain circles of agriculture, a sector that was especially distressed by the economic crisis.

In 1930, farm owner Knud Bach initiated the formation of an association to defend agricultural interests with all means necessary. In a short time, the Farmers Association (Landbrugernes Sammenslutning, or LS) grew from being a small, local association in the vicinity of Randers to become a nationwide organization with political views that were highly critical of the "system". The "system" was LS's umbrella term for the parliamentary democracy and the leading institutions of society: The government, the Folketing and Landsting, the political parties, the unions and other trade organizations. The "system" was blamed for driving the farming industry into the economic crisis and causing so many enterprising farmers to give up their farms and end in foreclosure.

In 1935, the management of LS organized a demonstration that received overwhelming support and for that reason attracted considerable attention. On Sunday, July 28, the participants of the Farmer's Procession had come to the capital from all over the country, and when they gathered at Amalienborg Palace Square the following day, the authorities estimated that around 40,000 were people present. It was their intention to seek out the King, have him circumvent the "system" and take the initiative to help the distressed farmers realize the very economic and political demands that had recently been adopted by LS at their general meeting. The tone was threatening, and although the democracy hardly faced any imminent danger of a fascist inspired coup, the King had nonetheless been placed in an extremely difficult situation. He obviously couldn't ignore the fact that so many people had gathered on the square, nor could he engage in matters of a political nature.

At 10 a.m., the entire royal family came out on the balcony, and the King made a short speech about the difficult times for town and country and said that the time had come to concentrate on the mutual tasks at hand. The King's "Long live Denmark" was met with resounding cheers followed by "Kongesangen" (The King's Song), after which the King met in his study with a delegation led by Knud Bach. Christian X had made sure that Prime Minister Stauning would also be present, and after the demands had been made, the King said that while he had not refused to meet with the delegation, he, as a constitutional king, had to pass on the claims to the population's legally elected representatives.

By mid-afternoon, the Farmer's Procession left Amalienborg Palace Square in a quiet and orderly fashion. The mood was high, and the King received much praise, though likely it was difficult to hide the fact that he so cleverly had avoided getting involved in the political troubles.

Gunfight at Amalienborg

With the army disbanded after the collapse of the policy of collaboration on August 29, 1943, it became the responsibility of the police to guard the Danish residential palaces. The following summer, a spontaneous general strike had sparked violent riots in the streets of the capital, causing further augmentation of the Amalienborg Guard to a total of fifty-six soldiers.

Tuesday, September 19, 1944, began as a beautiful, sunny day in the capital. Late in the morning, as was often the case, the air alarms sounded, indicating an imminent air raid, and people went indoors and waited patiently to see what would happen. But the characteristic sound of low-flying bombers never came. It had been a false alarm, launched by the occupation forces to serve as a cover for a large-scale operation against the police all over Denmark. The personnel of the many local police stations were quite simply arrested and interned, while an outright military attack was launched at the police headquarters in Copenhagen. The Germans, however, had no plans to relieve the Amalienborg Guard, but when the police officers on duty at the royal residence learned what was happening at the police headquarters and around the country, they decided to put up a fight.

After a brief consultation with his adjutant, Christian X had ordered that no unauthorized persons were to enter the square. Following that, barricades were built in haste and chevaux de frise placed by the Colonnade and the three other entrances to the square. At Toldbodgade, German guns threatened to open fire on the palaces, and when a platoon of German marines from Sankt Annæ Plads began advancing toward the Colonnade, orders were given to beat off the attack. The shooting began, and three hours of fighting passed until a telephone message from SS-Obergruppenführer Pancke came in, ordering the attack on the dwellings of the Danish King to be stopped immediately. The attack had been a mistake.

Eleven German soldiers—but no Danish police officers—had lost their lives, and both sides had several wounded. Among these was the palace steward, Captain Schlichtkrull, who had been shot in the abdomen while trying at the beginning of the attack to get in touch with the leaders of the advancing German platoon. At a subsequent negotiation it was agreed that the task of keeping guard at Amalienborg should remain in the hands of the Danish police.

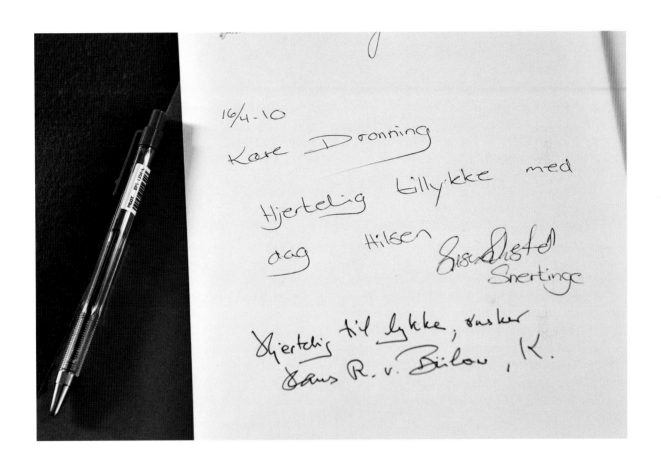

16/4-10

Kære Dronning

Hjertelig tillykke med
dag Hilsen Sisse Østed
Snertinge

Hjertelig til lykke, ønsker
Hans R. v. Bülow, K.

The Centre of the Monarchy

Interview with Queen Margrethe II

To the Queen, the Amalienborg palace is not just a home, but also the headquarters of the Court. She has experienced national events unfold here since childhood, and looking forward she believes that Amalienborg will remain the centre of the monarchy.

"Why are they cheering? It's not grandpa's birthday!" That's what first occurred to the princess when the sounds of voices from the street woke her up. It was spring, and though she was only five, she was old enough to know that grandfather's birthday wasn't until autumn. Heavy with sleep, princess Margrethe was awakened by the euphoria on the evening of the liberation on May 4, 1945. The palace square was blocked off, but once the liberation message had been broadcasted on the radio, people spontaneously flocked to Amalienborg, and since they couldn't enter the square, they lingered in the very streets under the windows of the princess's room. This was the culmination, the unforgettable days, when the German occupation of Denmark and the dark years of war finally came to an end.

The Queen recalls these particular days as being confusing and strange. She had the experience of sitting in the palace basement the following day, on May 5, when there was shooting from Holmen on the other side of the harbour entrance. Initially, Margrethe and her younger sister, Benedikte, were brought to the part of the first floor that didn't face the harbour, but later the parents, Crown Prince Frederik and Crown Princess Ingrid, decided that this wasn't safe enough.

"At this point," the Queen says, "things apparently became a little bit too much, and my parents thought we'd better move to the basement."

A strange atmosphere, alternating between joy and worry, prevailed in the basement where the parents and daughters stayed. The parents realized that though the war years were now past history, no one knew what to expect from the peace. Normally, the Queen was afraid of loud noises as a child, but not at this time; she had been shielded from the dangers of war, and perhaps she could sense that her parents had no real fear of any devastating impact, even though bullets whizzed through the air. Denmark had made it through the war without bloody battles and massive bombings, and everyone hoped that it would not end in disaster this late in the war. "There had been very few bombings of Copenhagen, and the adults were not that afraid. There had been the terrible incidents in late March, the bombings of the French school and the Shell House, and other operations had been carried out at the Burmeister & Wain shipyard. But we got off mercifully at home and nobody had the terrifying fear of a person who has experienced being bombed and wonders, 'How will it be tonight?'"

The Royal Guard Marches In

These flashes of Liberation Day live on in the Queen's memory—the happy voices from the street, the hours in the basement—but they are not her only memories from the time when Denmark became a liberated country. She remembers her father showing her the Royal Guard marching into the

Palace Square for the first time since the end of the war. Having listened quite often to march tunes on her father's phonograph, it was almost as if she knew the soldiers, and she was also the proud owner of the picture book, With The Guard Through the City. "I knew how The Royal Life Guards looked, even though I had never seen them in reality. During the war, they stood guard in the gray uniforms until they were relieved by the police, so it was exciting to witness the guard making its entrance again."

Even if she saw things through the eyes of a child, she did sense the euphoria of Liberation Day. People crossed the square to greet her father and mother. She knew that Grandma had met Montgomery, the British general, who had been applauded as he drove through Copenhagen. She also remembers the special atmosphere when the flag at Christian VIII's palace, where her grandparents lived, was about to fly at full mast again. To better see the palace, her grandma came to visit so she could look directly across at her home and enjoy the sight of the flag being raised and then unfold. "She wanted to see this with my father," the Queen recalls.

Headquarters

In the following years, she participated in countless events at Amalienborg—birthdays, New Years banquets, balls, visits by government leaders and heads of state from all over the world—and when she herself became monarch, the palace became her headquarters.

Each year she travels with the Prince Consort between the various family homes. In the summer they live at Fredensborg Palace and also stop by at Gråsten Palace, and around Christmas they move to Marselisborg Palace in Aarhus. But the centre remains Amalienborg. The Queen has her office at the palace where she conducts meetings with her advisers. When guests arrive, she will see them in the reception room. The Queen's father worked in much the same way when he was King. When the family resided at Fredensborg Palace, he drove to town to meet with the cabinet secretary, just like Queen Ingrid drove to town when she was planning events. "This is how things have worked after the introduction of the automobile. Previously, everything more or less had to be moved to where the King was, but not any more." With Amalienborg serving at the same time as home and office, it can be difficult at times to determine when one function turns into the other, when work is superseded by leisure—and vice versa.

This has gradually become a lifestyle, and the Queen couldn't imagine any other way of working: "Under no circumstances do we work nine-to-five. We work when we work; sometimes it's much more than eight hours, sometimes not quite that much. Occasionally, one will take a vacation, but the person and the function are two sides of the same coin, one essentially works all the time. That, at any rate, is how I see it."

The 70th Birthday

To most Danes, Amalienborg is synonymous with the royal family. On any given day, it's a beautiful edifice to be admired by Copenhageners who happen to pass by. On the Queen's birthday, however, the palace takes on a new dimension, becoming the formidable setting of the Court and the monarchy. And lots of Danes participate.

The Queen celebrated her 70th birthday on April 16, 2010, and the Danes beat a path to the palace square. Eventually the crowd got so packed that people had to give up and merely stay in the side streets. From the balcony the Queen looked across a surging sea of faces with the Dannebrog banner waving in their hands. Some people might find it appealing to wave to a crowd from a balcony, and seen from the outside it does seem manageable to take this small step onto the balcony, but the Queen felt like she was crossing a ravine the first time she was at the centre of such overwhelming attention. Not that she hadn't practised on the sly; she had her "debut" while still a baby, in 1940, and she vaguely remembers King Christian X's birthday in 1942, and how she stood on the balcony next to the King. She remembers his tall, black riding boots—boots as tall as she—and how scary they were.

She would stand on the balcony many times with her parents, but being the centre of attention was dramatic. That day arrived in 1958 when she turned eighteen. "It was a quite overwhelming and intense experience. My father helped and said, "When people wave and shout hurray, remember to receive it. Do it like this!" says the Queen, demonstrating with her hands her father's imitation of an embrace.

The Importance of Showing Joy

The King wanted the Danes to know that their greetings went straight to his heart and that he was grateful for their attendance, and now he tried to teach his daughter the same simple

gesture. "It was hard, but I did understand what my father meant. He had an amazing ability to embrace people in a natural way. He showed me that I had to reach out to people and not retreat into myself. He showed me that it was a warm exchange between the people on the square and those of us up there on the balcony, something I've felt to this very day."

Nevertheless, it was almost too much, and the Queen has since witnessed Crown Prince Frederik struggle with the same shyness. "Ask the Crown Prince how it was," laughs the Queen. "He too felt it quite overwhelming the first time." The decisive change for the ruler came at the time when her shyness gave way to the joy of being able to greet the Danes and when she had worked up the courage to be at the centre of attention in a natural way. "Around the time when I got married it became easier to receive. I clearly sensed the warmth, and that's something a person would like to reciprocate. I feel that it's important to display how happy and grateful one is that so many people show up."

These days, the Queen looks forward to the event and no longer has to fight the urge to run inside and hide behind the curtains. "I definitely think this is something special. It most certainly is not anything that one just needs to get over with. It's truly a joy."

The New Year's Address

The Queen also delivers her New Year's address from Amalienborg. Without stepping forward physically, she speaks directly to the Danes through cameras and microphones lined up in the study. The New Year's address is a ceremony that the majesty gives careful consideration and many hours of work each fall. The respect for the task and the meticulous care for each and every word are probably the reasons why the speech for most people is a must-see. It's not a proper New Year's Eve if one doesn't begin by gathering in front of the television when the image of Amalienborg appears, and shortly thereafter a cut is made to the majesty, sitting behind the desk. This is where she delivers the speech—directly and without a safety net—unlike the prime minister's address from the official residence at Marienborg, which is a pre-recorded speech that can be redone prior to the broadcast. When the Queen begins, most living rooms fall silent, diligent people in the kitchen pause for a while, children are shushed, and the volume is turned up a bit so everyone can hear the words.

The Speech is a Paradox

In many ways the speech is a paradox in a modern media world of constantly increasing pace and broadcasters struggling to attract the viewers' attention with new concepts that rarely keep thoughtfulness and reflection as their first priority. And yet there is room for a transmission that opens with an elderly lady who unfolds her eyeglasses, placed them on the nose and beings to read from her sheets of paper.

This is how the Queen has delivered her speech year after year; ever since she, forty years ago looked into the camera lens and began her first speech. At no point has the audience decreased, and that so many choose to listen to the New Year's address is significant, not in the least for the one delivering the speech. "The speech is very important to me, as it

was to my father. We used to always watch on television while he delivered the speech in the adjacent room. When it became my turn, it was quite a handful. It was obligating and exciting. Gradually it has become a speech that people want to hear, and that makes it even more of an obligation, but it's certainly also a great joy," says the Queen. Like that first step onto the balcony, delivering the maiden speech was like jumping off of a ledge, without knowing where one could get a foothold. "I don't even remember what I said, but I remember being really anxious. I wouldn't say that I was trembling with nerves, but from the pictures I can tell that I was like a coiled spring."

Intensive Preparation

Prior to delivering the speech, the Queen goes through a long process, and the final speech is the result of a close cooperation between the Court and the Ministry of State. The process begins with the Ministry of State submitting the first draft to the Queen. "I always get a draft that I work from. There may be larger or smaller differences between what is proposed and what I end up with. It varies somewhat, since no other person would have any way of knowing how I want to express things, but they come with a suggestion, and that's the text I work with in cooperation with the cabinet secretary. This process ensures that we end up with a thoroughly prepared text. I always try to include in the speech something that I want to express and emphasize on this particular New Year's Eve."

In other words, the Queen prefers to focus on new messages from year to year, or as she phrases it herself—it's not

pleasant "to feel that you are quoting yourself." Reading the speeches, one will discover the Queen's wide thematic range. She will touch upon the same overall themes as in the speech delivered by the head of government the following day, on January 1, reflecting national and international developments, but she always has her own distinctive message and choice of words that gives the speech personality. At times she will give her speech more edge and talk about the "smart-alecky comments" of the Danes, or mention a hunt for eternal youth that denigrates life experience and wisdom. "I want to say something that is on my mind and that will mean something to people, and at the same time it must have a connection with the past year. On the other hand, I don't wish for the speech to become too topical. That's not the aim of a New Year's address. Nor should it be political, but that to me is second nature. It has to be something you truly believe and something that you hope people will be able to receive and take to heart."

The speeches have, on several occasions, launched public debates. In some cases the Queen knew that her words would cause a stir, but in other cases the reactions took her by surprise. "Sometimes one might have suspected that a certain message would get some attention—and then nothing happened—while at other times one might have thought: 'By God, was what I said really that curious!'"

Cooperation with the Prime Minister

The work, as mentioned, is not done with a completely free hand. The Queen will make her significant marks on the speech, but it's the responsibility of the incumbent prime minister to ensure that the majesty does not cross the border and become political. According to the Constitution, she must be non-liable and not interfere directly in politics. "When I have made my draft of the speech, it returns to the prime minister. No official speech is made without the prime minister knowing its content, and it might well be the case that the prime minister proposes a slightly different phrasing. One does of course take note of that."

Conversely, the Queen is of the belief that the speech must never be so diplomatic as to become too smooth and trivial. "It should never end up being what my father called 'lirumlarum' or 'tittle-tattle and small talk'. When people sit down to listen, they deserve that something is being said."

The exact limits of what the Queen is allowed to say is a well kept secret. A qualified guess would be that there are no visible boundaries, which the Queen herself is aware of: "Unfortunately, it depends to a large extent on the eyes of the beholder. Out of the blue someone will claim that I have been political in a particular part of the speech, while it's clear to others that it certainly was not my intention. Each time someone felt that I was a little too political, I have fortunately always sensed that others said, 'Of course she can say that!' I do trust that the prime minister would stop me if I went too far. On the other hand, if I were to write speeches without ever running the risk of being told to watch out a bit, then I would never be able to say anything."

For the Queen, however, it's an absolute rule not to touch upon anything that is "specifically party political." She should never become part of the political struggle at Christiansborg. "This is not about whether or not one particular party might have ideas that are consistent with one's own. If you never corresponded with anyone, you would have no ideas. On the other hand, obviously one can have views that one would never dream of talking about outside the house—and these views of course never make it into the speech. I have my views, but only for personal use. Above all, the New Year's address concerns my country. That is what the speech should be about."

The Long Haul

The same guiding principle is echoed in the Queen's views regarding the position of the Court in society and its position in relation to the political life unfolding at Christiansborg. "In my view we represent something that goes beyond the day-to-day political issues—or so we should. We should accentuate something about the country in general, about how the country looks at the given moment, while at the same time be a thread to the past and perhaps to the future. I believe it to be the obligation and strength of any monarchy to represents continuity. We are not a flash in the pan, nor is our country."

From the Queen's perspective, this is the lifeblood of the Court. She is committed to ensuring continuity and roots, and she is well aware that this is a delicate balance. "The fact that it has been passed from generation to generation is a big opportunity. You know your role. You know what you can do, what you can't do, and what to stay away from. And this I believe to be extremely important: Representing continuity without participating in the everyday struggle. I do also think that my two sons and my daughters-in-law understand this rather well, and I think it shows."

The Queen has never lectured her sons about the task of being royal. With her example she has tried to strike the preliminary notes. "I don't think I have ever preached. I've tried to give it to them along the way, in the same way it was given to me. I don't remember my parents ever giving me a curtain lecture or a reading about how it should be done. It came gradually. That's how it works when things are passed on from generation to generation." Ideally, the next

monarch should develop a certain degree of empathy and be endowed with an understanding of the specific country. "I believe that all royal houses of Europe, when they look at one of the other countries, will say to themselves: 'Thank goodness, I'm not there!' But it's different when you have grown up in a specific place and you're in harmony with this country. If one were to look at the other countries from the outside, one would say, 'My God, I would never know how to do that.' And nor do I have to."

Continuity

For the Queen, a large part of the art of being a ruler has to do with the ability to be contemporary and in harmony with the age—without succumbing to it. "One should be aware of what is in vogue, but one should also be aware that what might seem so important today could dwindle to nothing in ten days. In other words, one should not follow the trend of the times—to use an expression I actually hate. It may be that I'm an old woman, but whether it's about sweaters or opinions, I don't think anyone should allow themselves to be dictated by the fashion of the day."

It's crucial to have the ability to distinguish between the whims of today and the long haul. "No one knows anything about the future, but I see no reason as to why we shouldn't continue. I believe it's good for a country to have the perspective embodied by the royal family. There will always be continuity, but with someone who can represent that continuity while being capable of staying out of politics, I certainly believe that we have a future.

THE SPEECH TO THE NATION

At the New Year's banquet on the first day of 1941, the Queen's grandfather, Christian X, went to the microphone for the first time to convey on the radio his New Year's wishes to the Danish people. "The times are grave and heavy," he said in his speech that lasted less than three minutes. The old horse-riding King was a man of few words, and the following New Year's speeches broadcasted on the radio were even shorter.

In 1958, television had gained such currency in the population that the time had come to transmit images of the King's speech at the New Year's banquet. It took place at eight pm. between the fish and roast, and this arrangement turned out to be somewhat impractical. At any rate, the King—who by now was Frederik IX—decided that the speech henceforth no longer would be delivered at the banquet on New Year's Day. It was to be converted into a live radio and television transmission from the King's reception room at Frederik VIII's Palace on New Year's Eve at six pm. Even if King Frederik's speeches rarely contained more than well intentioned, quite formal New Year's greetings to those near and far, they did attract the attention of the population. Those were, after all, the King's words on the air.

However, they never commanded as much attention as the speeches of Queen Margrethe, who since 1972 has delivered far more comprehensive speeches in which the well-read and well-informed ruler through the years increasingly has sought—quite deliberately—to take this opportunity to express her personal reflections on important issues regarding the times, the community, and the surrounding world. In these speeches the Queen nonetheless complies fully with the formal rhetorical demands by sending her greetings to all parts of the kingdom, to Danes living out in the big world, to Greenland and the Faroe Islands, to the Danish minority of South Schleswig, to the Armed Forces and the Police, and those with hardships or grief to bear.

The Queen's speeches have not only become significantly longer, they have also evolved into being much more than eloquent pleasantries, and in this context they have frequently been the subject of both praise and criticism. She will often express herself with an abundance of imagery, and for this she was awarded the Danish Language Society prize in 1989.

While the Queen delivers the New Year's address, a group of leading
employees have their eyes glued to the screen, here Lord Chamberlain Ove Ullerup and Private Secretary Henning Fode (both seated);
behind them Master of Ceremonies Christian Eugen-Olsen.

The Right To Be a Child

Interview with Queen Margrethe II

While growing up at Amalienborg, Queen Margrethe felt that she was allowed to be a child. Today, it seems to her that the childhood of contemporary children becomes shorter and shorter, while at the same time people expect to be young all their lives.

It was a magical moment for the three princesses when the family gathered in the living room in the winter. The tall, arched windows let in the thin winter daylight from the palace square, and the fireplace in the corner kept the chill at bay. "During the dark times we sat by the windows, drinking tea," recalls the Queen. It filled her and her two sisters with a harmonious feeling to sit in the room with their parents. "At times father would read aloud to us. My mother didn't care much for reading aloud, but dad enjoyed it and was an expressive and funny reader." When the kids had been tucked in, Queen Ingrid and King Frederik usually spent the evening alone, but as the daughters grew older, they would often stay after dinner and listen to music with their parents.

Each year, the King would give private concerts as well as a few with the Danish National Symphony Orchestra (Radiosymfoniorkesteret) and the Royal Danish Orchestra (Det Kgl. Kapel). Around these times he would listen extra carefully to the classical music on the spinning record player. "He would listen while reading the score. He always made himself very familiar with the music they would be playing. At other times, he would put on a record and just listen to it with our mother, who was also fond of music." The same could be said for Margrethe, who at an early age fell in love with dancing. "When I was little, they often played records that were fun to move along with—and I would dash about the rooms and dance. I did this, even when I was quite small, and long before I went to the theatre. Music and motion has always seemed connected to me." Later in life, the Queen would regularly attend the performances of The Royal Danish Ballet and take up ballet herself.

Weekdays and Celebrations

When Queen Ingrid and King Frederik were busy with official affairs, the three princesses were surrounded by nannies, an arrangement that none of the princesses questioned. "They made sure we behaved, even when my parents were absent, and they made sure our clothes were in order and that our hair was nicely done—and all those things."

Though the nurses were popular, they couldn't compete with the parents, who played a vital role in the lives of the princesses. Looking back, the Queen recalls with pleasure weekdays|as well as special occasions. March was joyously anticipated, as this was the month where King Frederik and Queen Ingrid could celebrate their birthday only a few weeks apart. "Their birthdays were always so festive—my father's birthday was March 11, my mother on March 28. At this particular time, the flowers began to come out of the ground, and father and mother were always given lots of flowers. When I became old enough, I would often spend the morning help mother's lady's maid with putting flowers in water."

'I'll be damned if that's not Frederik'

King Frederik's 50th birthday in 1949 is an especially memory. "Like all other schoolchildren, we had the day off on Dad's birthday. I recall this day as a huge event. There were lots of people on the square, and Dad was so happy." King Frederik loved birthdays and looked forward to greeting the people from the balcony. "He liked it in a sweet and modest way. He was a shy man, but it pleased him to sense the genuine warmth of the people," recalls the Queen.

The King had returned to Amalienborg the day before his 50th birthday, and he was very cheerful. "He had gone for a ride around town, and passing through the Østerbro district, he at one point had to stop for a red light. A slightly tipsy gentleman was standing on a street corner. When he saw my father, he said, 'I'll be damned if that's not Frederik! Hello Frederik, happy birthday tomorrow!' My father could always tell when it was real, and he enjoyed this kind of contact."

Birthdays at the Palace

The birthdays followed certain traditions. "A birthday table was set up with birthday cake and candles in honour of the birthday child, whether it was my father, my mother or us

children. This took place early in the morning. Afterwards, my father usually held a reception with well-wishers coming by to congratulate him. Later a lunch would be served where family members would often participate, and I was almost always allowed to participate. When I turned nine, I began participating at the evening dinner when my father and mother's closest friends came over, and it was always festive."

While the princesses still attended school, the morning birthday celebration was moved a bit. "If we had class at eight o'clock, my parents felt that it was just a tad too early! We could stop by and say good morning, but setting up a birthday table was a little too much! So we postponed that part of the celebration until we were back from school, which made it twice as exciting." Queen Margrethe and the Prince Consort adhered to the same traditions with Crown Prince Frederik and Prince Joachim. When they returned from school, the parents had the birthday table ready.

Room to be a Child

The Queen has a happy recollection of the land of childhood. She cherished the sojourns at Fredensborg Palace, but also the winters at Amalienborg, where in particular the afternoons and evenings with the parents emerge as gold-tinted memories. But the perhaps most important thing was that she was given the space to pursue her interests. Even as a child she developed several of the interests she has been engaged in as an adult, and there's a direct line from her childhood love of drawing and painting to her later artistic work as a painter, set designer for theatre and dance performances, and the creator of imaginative decoupages.

Personal Space

Seen in retrospect, the Queen might have benefitted from the fact that several years passed before it became clear that she would be the Crown Princess. That fact was first established with the adoption of the Act of Succession in 1953. This law allowed so-called conditional female succession, paving the way for Margrethe's way to the throne. This reversal of the monarchy's succession rules dramatically altered her life and changed her fate forever. When she was young, the Queen experienced a period of unease after being so suddenly appointed to such a prominent position. In one stroke, she could no longer play the less demanding part of a princess who could sometimes hide in the wings. With the change of the rules of succession, Margrethe knew that one day she would have to step into the spotlight of the big stage where everyone's eyes would be fixed upon her, and she was not comfortable with that perspective.

In a 2003 interview with the British newspaper The Sunday Telegraph, the Queen spoke openly about how difficult it was, at age 13, to grasp the scope of the new role: "I was a late bloomer and very insecure growing up. My parents prepared me for my future role, but it was not easy. And I was not easy. Today, it seems to me that my insecurities and

discomfort were equal parts constitutional law and hormones." Fortunately, she later learned to believe that she could and should assume the task. She accepted and took on her destiny.

Gradual Preparation

While raising their oldest daughter, Queen Ingrid and King Frederik carefully prepared her to one day become the Queen of Denmark and the many obligations it entailed. They involved their daughter and let her witness how the task could be executed. It was "learning by doing", or perhaps rather "learning by seeing." The Queen calls it "osmosis"—the parents letting their knowledge and experiences ooze into their daughter. This undertaking by the parents turned out to be successful.

When King Frederik died after a brief illness in the winter of 1972, Margrethe felt a profound grief over her father's death while at the same time she had an inner strength, knowing to the bone that her father would have been proud to see her step forward as the ruler. At this time, she had come to terms with assuming the role of monarch and become the Queen of Denmark. And although her life since then has been filled with a wide range of obligations, ceremonies and rituals, she has always left room open to be an artist, and she has never lost the connection to the land of childhood. The child's right to be a child and how childhood influences the formation of a human being, is a theme that engages the Queen's attention.

The Land of Childhood

The Queen wishes for her grandchildren to have a childhood as free and happy as she experienced. This is one of the reasons why she strives to keep an intrusive press at a distance from the little princes and princesses. The Queen cares not only about her own. Generally speaking, she is both saddened and alarmed when children are prematurely squeezed into the established patterns and put in boxes that will shape them in one way or another. To the Queen, being a child is a human right and she disapproves of the tendency to reduce childhood to a parenthesis. "There is so much talk about children, about their conditions and rights, while curiously the years of being a child have been reduced compared to when I was a child." She emphasizes, however, that she is not attempting to romanticize the conditions of children at the time when she was a child. "I'm so old and hail from the days when country children only went to school for a few years before they went into domestic service. Nonetheless, they were children while they were children. The schooling system was different in the cities, yet the children were allowed to be children until their parents considered them mature enough to be adults."

The Queen has noticed that small children have begun to look like adults early on. "Today even little girls are dressed in fashion clothes, as if they were fifteen or seventeen years old. This, to me, is a strange development. In a way, these children are not allowed the right to be children—or not given the possibility—compared to how it

was in my time. We were not preoccupied with all this fashion stuff; we had plenty of other things to do. Naturally, many children today have a wonderful time, but still it's as if a part of childhood has been stripped away."

The Importance of Playing

The Queen dreads the idea of entering an era where children early on start to behave as a kind of semi-young or semi-adults. "It's the way of the world these days, and perhaps it will turn out that the generations where children were children, not little adults, was a short historical period," says the Queen. "The right to be a child was, I assume, only granted the generations of my grandparents, my parents, myself, and my children. I had a wonderful childhood, and that might be the reason why I wish for others to have a similar experience."

Naturally, the Queen is well aware that she was born into a life of privilege; still she maintains that childhood back then lasted longer—for her as well as for her peers of a more modest background. "They definitely didn't live under the same conditions as I, yet they had a happy and secure childhood where they were allowed to enjoy being children. They could play and have fun. One's childhood was given the necessary time to unfold."

Today it's common knowledge that children by way of play and imagination will discover interests they can pursue later in life. This aspect, however, does not have the Queen's focus. She finds that there is a special—and independent—value in the freedom of the child to explore the horizon without being led in a particular direction. "Some people will early in life find something that they care about, whether it's a hobby or something that will turn out to become a profession. Others will not find this until later in life. It varies from person to person. A big part of my childhood was filled with exciting things. I read books. I was interested in birds and archaeology. I found the world to be filled with things exciting that a person could explore. The childhood of today has become very short while in turn you are expected to be young all your life!"

Eternal Youth

The Queen doesn't hide the fact that she is somewhat puzzled by the many adults who desperately strive to stay young. She believes that one should not be subject to this fixation on eternal youth, and at the same time she battles the tyranny of age. This perhaps has something to do with her growing up with relatively old parents, who by their own example demonstrated that the mere date on the birth certificate shouldn't determine one's curiosity and zest for life. "My parents never seemed old to me. At times I even felt that my friend's parent were much older," says the Queen. Even as their skin became wrinkled and their physical strength waned, Queen Ingrid and King Frederik were very much alive and present. It strikes the Queen that many of today's adults seem so busy staging themselves as young while greeting the world with rigid minds and tired eyes.

Being There for the Child

In the Queen's view, adults often fail to be there for the children at those very times in their lives when they are most eager to learn from the adults. "In my childhood and youth I had the privilege that people always listened to me and answered my questions. I probably experienced this more so than other children, and it's no secret that I have enjoyed this privilege my entire life. Children growing up today seem to get much of their knowledge from a computer screen. Granted, there is much to be learned this way, but it's a valuable thing to have an adult share their knowledge and experiences with a child, and we should not let this be forgotten. It's not just about 'how the world was when grandma was a child', it's about providing answers to such questions as what happens when the sun goes down—and all these other questions that children wonder about. Later, one must remember to answer the more serious questions that a young person might ask."

OUR LIFE GUARDS ON FOOT

The Royal Life Guards consist of a music band, a corps of drums, and armed troops. The Amalienborg Palace is inextricably linked with the Royal Life Guards, and it's been this way since the royal family moved into the palace after the Christiansborg Palace fire in 1794. There is always a security guard present, adequately armed to ensure that no one gains unauthorized access to the ruler. One could argue that modern technology could secure the head of state in more contemporary way. Yet it is unlikely for the soldiers guarding the entrances to the four palaces to be replaced, anytime soon, by surveillance cameras, computerized locks, or other hardware; their presence at Amalienborg is much more than a practical measure.

For many locals, the Life Guards marching through the city at noon is part of the city's soul, like the bells sounding from City Hall's tower, or the squeals from Tivoli's roller coaster. The changing of the guard, an old tradition upheld with its fixed rituals, adds to the square's special fairytale atmosphere on weekdays and for celebrations. Here, past and present go together in harmony, and the history of the Life Guards is both long and varied.

In the summer of 1658, Frederik III ordered his commander, Hans Schack, to organize an army unit by the name "The King's Regiment of Guards of Foot," and Frederik Ahlefeldt was appointed colonel of the troops (From 1661 and the following two hundred years, a royal life guard on horseback also existed). Only one month later, the Life Guards Regiment was engaged in its first battle of life and death. The Swedish King Karl X Gustav had gone ashore on Zealand with one of the largest armies in Europe, and they now marched toward the capital. The Life Regiment was headquartered in the Citadel, and this was the place from which the capital was defended during the siege and the subsequent assault on Copenhagen on the night between February 10 and 11, 1659.

The regiment consisted of enlisted soldiers who were skilled in the military profession. In peacetime, they could be put to use anywhere in society, and the troops were ordered to assist at construction sites, excavations and wherever cheap labour was needed.

After a few years, the soldiers of The King's Life Regiment were dressed alike in red jackets, red capes, short red pants, and felt hats. At a later point, the red shirt was replaced with a yellow one, decorated with an abundance of buttons. It had to be distinguished and posh. Christian V ordered the Regiment to be regarded as "Our Guard on foot—and always keep and retain the name thereof". A proud Frederik IV had had his life guards demonstrate their prowess at a parade, after which the private secretary of the British diplomatic representative wrote: "They were the best soldiers in the world, and nowhere will you find people more beautiful. They drill excellently".

Those were big words, and in the eighteenth century, the "world's best soldiers" were often rented out to foreign princes who were engaged in wars all over Europe. During the short

reign of Struensee (the power hungry royal physician to the mentally ill Christian VII) the doctor somehow managed to disband the Life Guards. This happened in January 1772, but as his downfall came only fourteen days later, it was the King's first order to have the Life Guards re-established and to accommodate them in barracks by the Rosenborg Palace. In the late eighteenth century, a several hundred meter long drill pavilion was erected along Gothersgade. It was later demolished during the inter-war period because of the widening of Gothersgade. Along with the introduction of new uniforms came the distinctive bearskin caps in 1805. Then came the wars—first the War with England, then by mid-century the Thirty Years War in Schleswig-Holstein, and later the defeat at Dybbøl, resulting in the painful loss of southern Jutland. All of them were moments of destiny, and all of them had the Royal Life Guards in the field.

This was also the case on April 9, 1940, when German troops marched through the streets of Copenhagen. At five fifteen a.m., the guard at Amalienborg were ordered to put up resistance, but they capitulated soon thereafter and the German advance at Amalienborg stopped and the firing ceased. "A deep sense of sadness, bitterness and shame seized me," wrote Lieutenant General Prior later, putting to words what many felt on that occasion.

During the years of the Occupation, the swastika flew at the Royal Life Guards barracks. After the Second World War, the soldiers have served as Army combat troops in connection with Denmark's international involvements under the auspices of NATO and the UN, most recently in former Yugoslavia, Iraq and Afghanistan.

THE GUARDS PARADE

Every day at 11.30 a.m., the parade marches from the barracks at Rosenborg through the city streets to Amalienborg. It usually follows a fixed route through Rosenborggade, Købmagergade, Østergade, Kongens Nytorv, Bredgade, Sankt Annæ Plads and Amaliegade. They arrive a little before noon at the palace square where changing of the guard takes place. When the Queen and Prince Consort are in residence, or when one of their sons is reigning in absence of the Queen, either the Corps of Drums or the Band of the Royal Life Guards will accompany the guardsmen through town.

The changing of the guard is a ceremony that varies depending on where the royal family is residing. It has three categories. At a "King's Guard", the guards leave the flag and the drum beside the Colonnade between the palaces of Christian VII and Christian IX, indicating that the Queen is residing at Amalienborg. The "Lieutenant Guard" leaves only the drum visible at the Colonnade and is exercised in the Queen's absence, and when the Prince Consort, Crown Prince Frederik or Prince Joachim resides at the palace. Finally, the "Palace Guard" has neither flag nor drum visible by the Colonnade. This type of guard is used when Amalienborg is uninhabited by any member of the royal family. On these

occasions, the Guard follows a shorter route through the city and has no musical accompaniment.

The Guard stays at Amalienborg for twenty-four hours, until it's replaced by a new shift. The replacement of the individual sentry follows its own specific pattern. The relief patrol will walk the square every two hours—first at 12-noon, then at 2 p.m. and so forth, throughout the day. After the guardsmen have been on duty for two hours they subsequently stay four hours in the guardroom before they again have to stand post on the square or in the backyards behind the palaces.

The red sentry box has been a characteristic of the Royal Life Guards since the opening of the first Christiansborg Palace in 1740. The boxes are positioned in pairs by all the doorways at Amalienborg as well as by Court palaces in the provinces where the Royal Life Guards are assigned. Fredensborg Palace has served as a residence since 1863, Marselisborg since 1902, and Gråsten Palace since 1935. On special occasions, Christiansborg Palace will also have guards assigned.

THE UNIFORMS

Though the current apparel goes far back in history, the uniform of the Royal Life Guards has changed quite a bit over the years. The blue trousers with the broad white stripes down the side were introduced in 1822, and the dark blue jacket, used for ordinary duties, in 1848. The red full dress uniform hails from the regiment's earliest period and is used for the Queen's birthday, for state visits and on festive occasions where gala is appropriate. The characteristic black bearskin cap was introduced in 1805. Fifty years later, the sabres became part of the Guards' military equipment. Allegedly they were spoils of war from the Three Year War (1848-50), although they are of French origin. The Germans had captured them half a century earlier at a time when Napoleon's armies seized most of Europe.

In 1903, the Royal Life Guards was issued different uniforms for guard and field duty. The current battle fatigues and service uniforms were introduced in 1984, while a dozen years ago a special desert uniform was created for troops posted abroad.

THE COLOURS

The Colours are an important element of the guard duty at Amalienborg. Originally they accompanied the soldiers in the battlefield where a fight for life and death was fought and where the fate of the kingdom was determined. These days they hold more symbolic meanings and bear the Life Guard motto: Pro Rege Et Grege—for King and People.

The Royal Life Guards is in possession of two gala Colours and a number of Guard Colours, the two oldest of which were an accolade from King Christian VIII in 1847. Two additional Guard Colours were donated by King Christian X in 1924 and Her Majesty the Queen in 1983.

The Queen has also bestowed the current regimental flag. In all, the Royal Life Guards is in possession of seven Colours, each of which carries three battle honours with the names of selected battles that the Royal Life Guards has participated in.

The symbolic meanings of the colours are a significant part of the Life Guard self-image. Here a colour bearing the Queen's monogram is returned to Christian IX's Palace.

AN ADJUTANT IS ALWAYS PRESENT

When the Queen is in a public space, a military person—the adjutant on duty whose rank is major or commander—is always part of her entourage. Her Majesty the Queen's Adjutants is an institution with roots far back into autocracy and it serves as a formal link between the Royal Household and the Defence. It is, in principle, the same institution as was determined by decree of January 20, 1808,

though the function, concurrently with the society's general development over the past centuries, has changed along with many other aspects of the Court.

The ongoing dialogue between the Defence and the Queen takes place via this link, and it's the duty of the Head of the Queen's Adjutants, Colonel Henning Brøchmann Larsen, to keep the Queen informed about everything that happens in the Defence. The Queen's Adjutants must furthermore ensure the guarding of the palaces where the Queen resides. The Royal Life Guards will set up and train the soldiers for the guard service, but as soon as the guardsmen leave the Gothersgade Barracks, they are under Brøchmann Larsen's command. He manages the Guard and maintains the external security of the places where the Queen is staying—at Amalienborg, Fredensborg, Marselisborg or Gråsten. This takes place in collaboration with the Commanding Officer of the Royal Life Guards. The personal safety of Her Majesty is the responsibility of The Danish Security and Intelligence Service.

The Cosmopolitan at Amalienborg

Interview with the Prince Consort

The Prince Consort has more strings to his bow than most people and has been the Queen's closest supporter and advisor over the years.

Raindrops. That was what greeted him at Kastrup Airport after the flight from sunny southern France, yet it's the warmth he remembers the most. Numerous Danes had come to welcome Henri Marie Jean André Count de Laborde de Monpezat, the unknown French diplomat and Princess Margrethe's husband-to-be. "All of them had come to see the giraffe—as the Danish saying goes—and I was the giraffe! It was raining, so I made a wet entrance, yet I felt the warmth of the people as they waved and cheered. I will always remember that welcome," says the Prince Consort.

He had only a vague sense of the Kingdom Prior to his arrival. "I knew very little about Danish history and culture, until I realized I was getting married and would end up living in Denmark. I knew that Denmark had been a great power in the thirteenth and fourteenth century, and I knew Viking history. Most people know that the Vikings plundered French villages, but it's less known that they also settled down and married the locals. Normandy was named after the Vikings." France was indeed devastated by the Nordic warriors who seized power, and gradually a new people emerged, the Normans, as they called themselves after becoming French and Christians. The Normans means 'men from the north'.

Holberg and Kierkegaard

The prince also had a good deal of knowledge about the more civilized Danes. As a student, he had read texts of popular Danish writers as well the more exclusive thinkers, and he liked them. "I knew about Hans Christian Andersen who is well-known in most parts of the world. The Little Mermaid made a huge impression the first time I read it. It's a wonderful story." He found Holberg's satirical comedies amusing and was fascinated with Søren Kierkegaard. In an interview early on, Prince Henrik was asked about his knowledge of Danish culture. He mentioned Hans Christian Andersen, and the reporter nodded. Then he mentioned Søren Kierkegaard, which apparently caused confusion. "Pardon?" said the interviewer. "Søren Kierkegaard, the great philosopher," said Henrik. "Why, is he Danish?" said the interviewer. It must have given food for thought that the Frenchman, hailing from a nation celebrating original thinkers, seemed to know more about Kierkegaard than one of his future countrymen.

Bookworm and Pilot

Denmark's future prince soon began to acquire new knowledge, reading extensively about Danish history and culture, including books about the Court and the family he would become a part of. He openly admits that the language was a tough barrier, and one of the few things he regrets is not making more of an effort to master it. "The language was an obstacle for me. I mainly read about Denmark in French and English, and thus I acquired the knowledge of my new home

in languages other than Danish. I was interested in the Danish language and tried to learn it, but it was not easy for me and it took a long time."

He never, however, locked himself up in his study. He enjoyed travelling the country and he has seen Denmark as few others have. As a pilot he crisscrossed Denmark's few square kilometres, and this gave him a new perspective on the country. "I flew around in my little aircraft—and you learn amazing things about a country when you fly low and can see everything so clearly." He would land on small airfields and get to know areas of Denmark away from Copenhagen and Amalienborg.

Land and Sea

It was hard at first to suppress his disappointment that there were no mountains—not as in Norway and Sweden and, of course, France. In Denmark, he had to travel to Bornholm to see cliffs and enjoy the dramatic sight of a rocky coast. Aside from that, proud ridges didn't characterize the landscape, and Denmark seen from the cockpit struck the pilot as flat indeed. He did, however, see a beauty that still fascinates him. "Denmark might be flat, but it's so green—and there is a rare interaction between the sea, the coast, and the ground. This sense of connectedness between land and sea makes Denmark a very special and beautiful place." Each year around springtime, he would look forward to the cruises with the royal yacht, Dannebrog, and the visits to Danish seaports. But it's one thing to know the country's physical environment and boundaries. Another and more important thing is the ability to face and understand the mentality that, for better or worse, exists in a country, and in this area he was no novice. Quite the contrary; he was international, global and cosmopolitan long before these concepts were fashionable. He had from his earliest childhood led a nomadic life that had exposed him to various different continents and cultures.

The Cosmopolitan

Henri de Monpezat was born on June 11, 1934 in the French town of Talence in the Gironde department, as the son of Count André de Laborde de Monpezat and Countess Renée de Monpezat. He spent the first five years of his life in Vietnam (then called French Indochina), where his father ran companies that had been founded by Henrik's grandfather by the turn of the century, including 40.000 square meters of coffee and rice plantations, as well as newspapers and other businesses.

Vietnam had been the home to a large part of the family before the Second World War, and when they returned after the war, most of the family property was still intact. Then, in 1954, France lost the fight against the communists, and the family was forced to leave, losing all their possessions in Vietnam.

It was a childhood and youth marked by big changes. In 1939, the family travelled back home to le Cayrou, the entailed estate in Cahors, where Henrik was taught at home until he in 1947 was enrolled at a strict Jesuit boarding school in Bordeaux, in itself a dramatic change of scene. He then went to secondary school in Cahors until 1950 when he returned to

Hanoi and graduated in 1952 from the French secondary school. Back in France, he studied law and political science at Sorbonne from 1952 to 1957, and Chinese and Vietnamese at École Nationale des Langues Orientales. In 1957, he once again went abroad to study Oriental languages in Hong Kong, and the following year he continued his studies in Saigon.

The Nomad

Nomadic life continued with his military service with the infantry in Algeria from 1959 to 1962. Following that he was employed by the Asia Department of the French Foreign Ministry, and from 1963 to 1967 he was embassy secretary at the French Embassy in London. In addition to French and Danish, the years abroad has made him proficient in English, Chinese and Vietnamese, and years of travelling he has given him an understanding of different cultures and he has learned to appreciate their differences.

His autobiography, "Destin Oblige" ("Destiny Obligates"), doesn't neglect the fact that if the wars had not led to a communist takeover, he might have ended up spending his life in Vietnam. Through the years he has maintained his love for the country. In late 2009 he went on an official visit to Vietnam along with the Queen, Crown Prince Frederik and Crown Princess Mary, and he took great pleasure in showing his childhood home—an ochre yellow house on a wide boulevard in the middle of Hanoi. Half a century earlier, the house had teemed with children and servants, a time so thoroughly engraved in the Prince Consort's mind that he can still sense

The dachshunds residing at Christian IX's palace are, no doubt, the most publicized and well-known in the country.

the smells and see the colours of his privileged childhood home of a bygone era.

French Roots

Apart from his love for Asia, the Prince Consort has deeps roots in France and enjoys returning to his second childhood country and the wine castle Château de Caïx in Cahors, where he also distributes his wines. It's beautiful country with South facing fields under a hot sun and the river Lot running by, irrigating the vines. His parents' final resting place is the family burial grounds at the small cemetery in the nearby village of Albas, and a big part of his family live in the surrounding area.

Cahors imbued the Prince Consort with a love for the ground and soil, and his respect for the gifts of nature originated in the frugal years, when the family became self-sufficient. In this French peasant country, he, as a boy, learned milking, churning butter, tending garden, skinning rabbits, butchering chickens and how to set up snares. He was taught all about what a man can do with his hands, and even today it delights him to see the crops grow, and he considers it a loss that so many people have forgotten what it's like to live on the countryside. "They have no idea how to boil an egg. Alors! And almost no one knows how to pluck a chicken, or skin a hare or a rabbit. Many will consider these things to be filthy, but they are realities, they are gifts," as he once stated in an interview with the Danish weekly, Weekendavisen.

While sojourning at Château de Caïx, the Prince Consort will walk the fields to see how the grapes ripen and participate in the wine production. That he loves this sanctuary is obvious to anyone who has witnessed the Prince Consort on his home turf. But it's not his place alone. It's important to him that his children and grandchildren feel connected to France. At the baptism of his grandchildren, he, in observation of family tradition, rubbed the children's lips with garlic and a drop of Jurançon and Cahors wine, a symbolic act to emphasize the kinship with France.

The Meeting

When considering the Prince's life, it's hardly a surprise that love would also be found on foreign soil. This took place while he was stationed as a diplomat in London. He has described the meeting in the preface of his memoirs: "One spring evening in 1965, a French diplomat left his apartment on Bryanston Square by London's Marble Arch. He was going to a dinner party with some friends. He was light-hearted, his tuxedo was pressed, his hair newly cut. A few days earlier he had been told that the Danish heir to the throne would be the guest of honour. He swore to leave this presumably rather starched company as early as decency would permit." These first lines describe an event he has later called an encounter with destiny. In his opinion, destiny is the only explanation as to how a Frenchman working in London as a diplomat would meet a visiting Danish Crown Princess. Furthermore, destiny had in store that they took to each other, fell in love, and managed to bridge the gap between their different worlds.

After this meeting, he remembered how he at age twenty-four had had his future told by a Chinese clairvoyant. The message had been that he, at thirty-three, would get married far away from his own country, and that he would disappear from the world—without dying. In this unknown country, he would re-emerge as the phoenix. His life would be exciting but with many pitfalls. The Chinese had also predicted that one year later he would lose a sister, which in fact did happen.

On June 10, 1967, he married his princess, and at the wedding in the Holmen's Church he became His Royal Highness Prince Henrik of Denmark. A year later, on May 26, 1968, Crown Prince Frederik André Henrik Christian was born. And on June 7, 1969, Prince Joachim Holger Waldemar Christian came into the world. Not long thereafter, his princess was pronounced Queen, which meant that, all at once, he had to come to grips with being husband, father, Prince Consort and citizen of another country—and all of this in public.

Though he did have quite some experience from the big world, no one could have prepared him for this sudden entry into a country so different from France, Vietnam and Britain, and no one could have schooled him in the role of being consort to the Queen.

Number Two

By marrying the Crown Princess, this proud man, who grew up in a patriarchal family, had to accept a life where he would be number two, and that has been a challenge. Before the wedding, the father cautioned his son against marrying. "You'll be skinned alive the rest of your days," he said. The son defied these words—and received his share of beating, scratches and bruises. The cohabitation of Prince Henrik and the Danes did for several reasons not progress harmoniously.

The Danish language was one stumbling block, and the newcomer was often ridiculed for his lack of proficiency, which was a tragedy for Prince Henrik, a man of so many linguistic skills. And the Danes have never realized that language is actually one of his greatest strengths. Another problem might have been that the Prince Consort at times expressed himself awkwardly on subjects that all Danes could relate to. The most famous quote—some would say infamous—dealt with his approach to parenting: "Children should be raised somewhat like dogs, with determination, consistency, and love". These words left many with the feeling that Crown Prince Frederik and Prince Joachim were kept on a very tight leash.

Messages of that kind were not welcome at a time when most people broke away from the 'Black School', and where the raising of children was more about negotiating than dictating. Finally, having to always stay one step behind his wife the Queen made the Prince Consort vulnerable. In the future it will be more and more common for men to have girlfriends and wives in more prestigious and better-paid jobs, but Prince Henrik was one of the first to be in that position. It was easy to ridicule a man who wore an admiral's uniform, but had to stand in his wife's shadow. Few realized that this man had actually been a soldier at war. The then star-interviewer of the Politiken daily, Ninka, once asked the Prince Consort what psychologically had been the most burdensome aspect of constantly being inferior to the Queen. He answered, "Not to be recognized as one hundred percent your own being".

In some of his poems—including one from Cantabile—he hints that living like barons and kings is not necessarily a life of happiness. In one poem he writes: "Narrow palace / Thousands of gates/ Room so scarce!" When the book was published he said that a person might have ten thousand windows and ten thousand rooms, but it's more about having one small room to yourself. He did emphasize that the poem first and foremost should be understood philosophically: "One might assume that a king is rich and can do whatever he wants; that everyone is looking at him and that he has money and benefits—and then the point, unpretentiously, is served in three short lines: If your mind is unable to go through the door and climb the wall, then living in a palace can be hard."

At one time, he made it unmistakably clear that at times he felt that his efforts were not appreciated. It was disclosed in a dramatic interview with the B.T. tabloid. The statements created a much debate and there was talk of a crisis at the Court. However, the royal family soon stood up for the Prince Consort, and in conversations with the journalist and writer Annelise Bistrup, the Queen has subsequently assumed some responsibility for her husband's crisis. She admitted that she had not always been sufficiently aware of his difficulties, that she had not always helped him enough—and that she was the one who wished that they spoke French in private.

The Queen touched on the subject in an interview not long before her 70th birthday: "I felt his support, but perhaps I forgot to reciprocate." In an interview before his mother's

---

Prince Henrik talking to Chief of Secretariat Mogens Christensen and Personal Secretary Olivier Lesenecal.

birthday party, Crown Prince Frederik also emphasized his father's importance to the Queen "They are like two pieces of a puzzle, perfectly shaped to fit each other. He has challenged her in her role as the Queen and as an individual." During his tribute speech to the Queen, Prime Minister Lars Løkke Rasmussen delivered the same message by making it clear that the Queen's husband had been an invaluable lifelong support to the Queen. The Head of Government spoke directly to Prince Henrik: "For that, Your Royal Highness Prince Consort, I give you thanks."

Perhaps the Danes have finally begun to take the Prince Consort to heart. The book "Solitary Man—Portrait of a Prince" by the journalist Stéphanie Surrugue showed the calibre of the Prince's personality. The book was well received. In the Berlingske Tidende daily, the literary editor, Jens Andersen, said book deserved to be read for, "clearing the way into a great and beautiful human being in an often very small and ugly country."

Denmark and the Danes

The Prince Consort speaks warmly of Denmark, but he can be sharp and direct when it comes to our less attractive character traits. "There is a Danish paradox. It's a country with big ideas, a country that is open to the world—trading is our livelihood—but in everyday life people often act as if they were trapped between four churches and three lakes. There's a tendency to jealousy, and it's as if we don't recognize the privilege of living in such a prosperous and safe country. At its worst, envy is almost a kind of a national trait of character."

But even if envy is one of the components of Danish character least favoured by the Prince Consort, his declarations of love are equally pronounced.

His love is not only for summer half-year with flickering sunlight on the coast and sea, nor for the long, light summer nights. These days he finds as much poetry in the dark hours of winter when the Danes seek refuge from the cold. He has grown fond of the Danish term "hygge"—spending some time indoor, surrounded by good friends, perhaps with a glass of beer or wine in hand. He finds the Danes to be a nation of uncomplicated people. "The charming thing about the soul of the Danish people is how easy it is to establish direct contact. The Danes are friendly, open-minded and straightforward. Life to us is a little lighter than it is for other people." The Prince Consort has not forgotten his first impressions of Denmark, or lost the knowledge that he gained after his initial arrival. "Denmark is rich in art and history. Today we are a small power, but Denmark used to be one of the leading nations of Europe. We should not forget that."

The Palace

Royal life has its privileges, but it also entails a number of challenges. This was one thing the Prince Consort realized when he and his wife set out to decorate and furnish their Amalienborg home. To him it was exciting as well as challenging to make a mark on the building in close collaboration with the Queen, and it turned out to be an advantage that the palace was in such bad condition.

"We were lucky. The palace had not been inhabited in two

generations and was fairly dilapidated. It had to be renovated, which meant that we could put our own stamp on it." The young couple joined forces and made a colourful break with the favoured pale and cool style of Danish design. "I say this with a smile, but at that time Danish interior decoration to me was cold and boring. It has changed, but when I arrived—a man from southern France and Asia—the colours struck me as very cold. The more I walked around here with my fiancée, the more boring everything seemed! The Danes didn't dare to use colours. Everything had to be the same everywhere. I do believe I shocked my wife a bit, but thankfully she ended up

not only accepting my sense of colour, she even liked the result."

When the Queen and Prince Consort decided to have no modern furniture at the palace, it was merely because of the room's proportions. The Prince Consort is a huge admirer of Danish furniture design. "There is a Danish tradition for furniture design of a very high quality. We are known worldwide for our modern furniture. They are beautiful and with uncluttered lines. We don't have that kind of furniture at the palace, though, but I do like them." Kaare Klint and Hans J. Wegner are among the favourites.

The Gardens

Besides having left his stamp on the design of the Amalienborg Palace, the Prince Consort played a bit role in arranging the private gardens behind the palaces and helped organize the gardens at Fredensborg Palace And he uses the herbs from the gardens in his cooking. Gastronomy is a major interest of his, and he is happy to acknowledge that not only has the meals of the royal family changed considerably, so has the eating habits of the Danish population. A varied cuisine and restaurants of international, even world class have replaced the old tradition with its endless amounts of potatoes and brown gravy. The Prince Consort has contributed along the way with his publications about food and wine. In the book "Absolutely Magnifique!" he restored a banquet of fifty-eight dishes that King Frederik III served at a party in 1668. In "Palate Delights", he introduced dishes from the French cuisine, and in "Château de Caïx" he tells about his wine, his wine castle and about favourite regional dishes of his childhood country.

The Art

The Prince Consort points out that no royal family merely live in the same palace. They are constantly travelling. "We are basically gypsies, luxury gypsies. We are on the move. We don't have one home. We have four, five or six homes, because we belong to the whole nation. This tradition isn't new. All the royal houses in Europe have done it this way."

In the Prince Consort's opinion, most human beings will find it both difficult and stimulating to have access to several homes. Because of the shifts, one has to be less concerned with the physical environment and focus more on the values and interests that one can bring along, and no matter where the Queen and Prince Consort are going, they always bring along their artistic minds. The Queen paints, illustrates and cuts decoupages, and the Prince Consort plays piano at an advanced level, creates sculptures, and writes. "Originally, music was my greatest interest. I've studied music since I was a child. I took piano lessons from when I was six years old, and it's fair to say that I played very well when I was eighteen or twenty years old. Since then it has gone downhill, but I can still play some pieces."

He has said in an interview that his mother thought he played well enough to try to get admitted to the academy of music. He auditioned and was accepted. "My mother said, 'Bravo, my dear son, you're a genius, but if you want to continue with this you have to practise the piano four hours a day. So if I were you, I would continue at the university…'"

Sculptures and Languages

For some years the Prince Consort made sculptures, a new artistic field where he managed to create almost thirty sculptures. At her 70th birthday the Queen was given a sculpture that had once been created by Prince Henrik but which was enhanced and cast in bronze. The sculpture depicts two people in a loving embrace.

Prince Henrik also has a love for words and languages, a subject he talked about with the journalist and author Bettina Heltberg in an interview when Cantabile was published, a collection of poetry that was praised by the French daily, Le Figaro. "I like French and Latin etymology; I like the search for what is behind the word. Suddenly, a three thousand year old word will take on whole new meanings. Words come to mean new things, and it happens especially fast these days. We use a word for a while, then it becomes worse for wear and takes on new meanings." Minstrel language has inspired the poetry, as has eighteenth century baroque and rococo, and other poets. "I have a preference for Baudelaire and Verlaine—they seem to suit my taste and temperament. I also like Aragon, Paul Éluard and Apollinaire, and I enjoy minstrel art and Renaissance writings. Someone called me an anarchist romanticist, and I guess that's fair enough."

The Prince Consort still writes and he can't give up the work with words. "Most people of my generation wrote a poem when they were eighteen or twenty years old, but I kept doing it. I don't have the time to write a novel, but I would like to." He has demonstrated his writing skills in several collections of poetry. However, the greatest Danish recognition came after the publication of his memoirs, "Destiny Obligates", which received beautiful notices in Weekendavisen, Berlingske Tidende, Jyllands-Posten and Ekstra-Bladet.

In Berlingske Tidende, Per Stig Møller acting as guest reviewer wrote: "Prince Henrik could easily have written some nice fairytale memories about how a French boy from Indochina won the Princess of Denmark. He could have written beautifully about his travels and about all the great men and women he has met while acting in an official capacity. They would no doubt sell. But Prince Henrik wanted more than just that. He dared to write ironically, compassionately, and in a meaningful and sarcastic way about his life and opinions."

Jyllands-Posten labelled them "exceptional royal memories" while Weekendavisen ruled that the book had literary qualities. In Ekstra-Bladet, Peter "Pedro" Christoffersen wrote: "Your Royal Highness has written an excellent, oftentimes brilliant, well-structured, amazingly frank, well-read, and intelligent book. Well, I believe that sums it up…"

Artistic Partnership

The Queen and the Prince Consort have at times joined forces in artistic projects—not that they normally keep their artistic interests separated. Quite the contrary; when it comes to her drawings and paintings, the Queen calls her husband her best critic. In return, she enjoys listening to his music, reading his words and watching him fashion his sculptures. They have studios at Fredensborg as wall as Amalienborg, and sometimes the Prince Consort will be polishing a bronze sculpture while his wife is cutting and pasting a decoupage. From where they work, they can see each other, but nobody talks; they are both fully concentrated on what that have in their hands.

The mutual preoccupation with art is a joy, says the

Prince Consort. "We meet in almost all areas, and we have a deep, common interest in literature, painting, sculpture and decoration. It's very fortunate, and maybe one of the reasons why our love is still so warm and alive."

Under the pseudonym H.M. Vejerbjerg, they translated Simone de Beauvoir's 'All Humans are Mortal' into Danish. The Queen has also illustrated the Prince Consort's books of poetry. In the early days of their marriage they amused themselves with composing nonsense verses, and there is a reason for this. In addition to the duties of the royal, they have always left some space to be spontaneous and playful. They share the same sense of humour, and loud laughter often resounds at the palace. In the summer of 2009, Prince Henrik offered a taste of this humour when Karen Margrethe Schelin of Berlingske Tidende visited him at Fredensborg Palace on the occasion of his 75th birthday. Everything went by the book. After the interview, the Prince Consort and the reporter went into the adjoining drawing room to offer the photographer an opportunity to capture the Prince Consort from new angles. The journalist spotted a beautiful, stuffed unicorn with snow-white fur, blue eyes, one hoof raised and a horn standing out straight from its forehead. "Why, that wouldn't happen to be a unicorn?" she exclaimed. "Yes, it's a unicorn," said Prince Henrik, "I shot it myself."

The Collections

On display at Amalienborg and Fredensborg is another of the Prince Consort's artistic interests. For years he has collected Asian, African and Inuit art. Before entering his study at

Amalienborg—where papers and books are piled up on the desk and a fire is crackling in the fireplace—one passes through a long hall with showcases placed by the window sections. This is his collection of jade from China.

"I've been interested in jade for a long time. These jades were offerings to the dead. Far back in time, upper class people were buried with these figurines. They brought all kinds of things along with them—bowls, guns, knives—things one assumed they might need. Some of these objects are ancient, dating back more than 2.000 years before Christ."

Holding the jade in his hands, the Prince Consort is imbued with excitement over the fact that the Chinese that far back in history could create such refined art from the hard stone. Due to the rapid development of China in recent years and the casting of foundations for new buildings and neighbourhoods, many tombs have been exposed and opened. "When you open a grave, you may find two hundred objects that can be sold at markets," says Prince Henrik, who has acquired most of the displayed jade over the last thirty or forty years. A small collection of animal figurines goes back to the family's years in Vietnam. "My parents had a fine collection of Asian art. My grandfather, whom I did not know, had a large art collection that unfortunately disappeared during the war. I've studied Asian art. I'm no expert, but I have some knowledge and take a deep interest in Asian, and especially Chinese art."

He furthermore has a collection of African and Inuit art at Fredensborg Palace. The Price Consorts finds that there is a connection between Inuit and ancient Mongolian art. "Inuit art has some of the same ideas and expressions that we find in the Mongolian Chinese sculptures going back to one thousand years before Christ. It's fascinating."

The Traveller

These are all aspects of the Danish Prince Consort, a man who has been in Denmark for so many years, and yet is known by only a few. Undoubtedly, many have explained this with him being from another country and with his difficulties in taking root in the Danish soil. But perhaps there is another explanation. While it's possible for him to be transplanted, he insists on retaining his temper and originality. He is not like most people.

In his book of memoirs he summarizes his life: "It's the nature of destiny to follow the most diverse paths. As a career diplomat I could have been sent to Tonga, Tananarive or Copenhagen to present my credentials. I still have all kinds of music in my head and could have studied music or composition. I could have withdrawn from the world and have devoted myself to the conjugation of ancient Yunnan verbs. I could have gone on adventures in the Gobi Desert and have run into the Danish Crown Prince, who criss-crossed the desert and lived in a tent for weeks. I might even be have met the Queen of Denmark by participating in excavations in the ruins of Palmyra. But by not making me a sedentary person, destiny has placed me forever in this beautiful Denmark and has lovingly surrounded me by the very people that I just might have imagined and in places where their destiny might have led them to meet me."

The Soft Power

*Trusted advisors collaborate closely
with the Queen and the royal family
on developing the Court and securing
its appeal to the Danes.*

It was not planned, nor did it comply with royal etiquette when 8-year-old Fatima threw herself at Princess Mary and hugged her. "I did it because she's cute," Fatima later told a BT reporter about the hug that caused the Crown Princess' security guard to smile and the lady-in-waiting to gape. Another little girl was equally enthusiastic. "I shook Mary's hand. Now I'll never wash my hand again!"

It is the summer of 2006. The Crown Princess has gone to Vollsmose, a neighbourhood that, in the words of the BT-reporter, is as infamous as Mary is famous. Of the neighbourhood's ten thousand people, seventy percent are of another ethnicity than Danish, and the area has been ripe with headline making riots, shots fired at police vehicles and stones thrown at firefighters.

The Crown Princess visited the neighbourhood for the first time with Crown Prince Frederik in 2004. She later expressed a desire to return and witness the everyday life of Vollsmose, but at her arrival, the district appeared transformed. Little girls wore their finest hair bobbles, songs at the morning assembly at the Hans Christian Andersen School sounded slightly better, smiling policemen rode on bicycles—and then, in the midst of it all, was the Princess in her horse and carriage. "This damn sure is the first time anyone's travelled by state coach around these parts," a

spectator said according to Ekstra-Bladet. Surrounding him were girls in headscarves, mothers and fathers, all of them holding their cell phones up high, ready to get a snapshot of Mary.

The same tabloid reported, "happy smiles and multiethnic idyll". "Mary, Mary, Mary, Mary!" chimed flocks of waving children. The Crown Princess met with a group of immigrant women, and the banister of the staircase to their apartment had been decorated with white bows. Berlingske Tidende reported how accompanying policemen allowed a flag-waving, motley crew of veiled women, prom-dressed girls, and Palestinian, Pakistani and Somali teenage boys with baseball caps turned backwards to get closer to Mary with their bouquets of flowers. "She's the Crown Princess, and she sure is nice-looking. I just had to see her," explained sixteen-year-old Omar.

A Glimpse of the Sun

Less than a year later, in the spring 2007, the Crown Princess visited the much-criticised Gellerup district of Aarhus, another place known mostly for its conflicts. Gellerup is usually referred to as a 'parallel society' where immigrants live without taking part in Danish society. This day was different. "Gellerup cheered for the Crown Princess," said a headline in the Jyllands-Posten daily that went on describe how Mary made the residents feel that they and their neighbourhood was a part of the Danish society. Everywhere she was greeted by cheering people who waited in the rain with their cameras and Danish flags.

"Mary's smile was a glimpse of the sun on a rainy day," was how Nicolai Wammen, the young mayor of Aarhus poetically put it. He stressed the high moral value of the visit, and how it helped residents, police and municipality in their mutual attempt to make integration work. "People of different ethnic origins in this neighbourhood are very impressed that it's possible to get this close to a royal person," said the mayor. BT reported how the very pregnant Crown Princess smiled and shook hands quite serenely while cameras flashed and the crowd jostled from all sides. In the words of Politiken, 'Mary shined on Gellerup'.

Soft Power

Visiting places like Vollsmose and Gellerup has added a new dimension to the royal family's travels in Denmark. Most people are familiar with the images of Queen Margrethe opening exhibitions, visiting nursing homes, and listening to the mayor's speech upon arrival. Or how the Dannebrog yacht, consolidating the realm, will call at ports along the coast of Denmark or embark on voyages to Greenland and the Faroe Islands. All of this is part of the royal family's effort stay in touch with the mood of the citizens and ensure a sense of solidarity regarding all things 'Danish'.

While the raw force of the monarchy is a thing of the past, the Queen and the royal family still manage to move around with authority and clout, and Danes flock to meet them. The visits of the Crown Princess to Gellerup and Vollsmose clearly demonstrate that it is not merely anoth-

er rock star or football player stopping by.

Princess Mary was not born in Denmark. She came to Denmark from across the globe, and perhaps that's one of the reasons why she can represent a Danishness that also appeals to people for whom it might be difficult to feel at home in Denmark, and who might in some cases even be opposed to what 'being Danish' implies. This is possible because the royal family has found ways to utilise a new form of power and influence.

The Queen and her family master 'soft power', as it is called in the United States. This kind of power is stronger than one might assume. 'Soft power' creates popularity and can make people support a particular idea, country, institution, or a person. The term, chiefly used within the areas of foreign and security policies, became more widely known after the 2004 publication of the book, "Soft Power: The Means to Success in World Politics", by Professor Joseph Nye of Harvard University. At the time, his analysis was seen as a counterpart to the George W. Bush administration's use of massive military superiority to win decisive battles in Iraq and Afghanistan, yet the administration struggled to win 'the fight for peace.' Essentially, the message is that one should not bet everything on military or economic supremacy, but rather that one must present an ideology, a culture or set of values that others might want to follow. The existence of the Danish royal family is to a large extent based upon a 'soft power' that, when successful, creates a unique sense of community. An editorial in Berlingske Tidende put it this way: "The hereditary monarchy is quite obviously a phenomenon that conflicts with

the fundamental democratic idea that all people are created equal. Why the Queen is the queen can't be justified rationally. But there are plenty of things with no rational justification. Why is it called Denmark? Why is the flag red and white? There are no rational reasons, yet like the monarchy, all these things are part of our identity."

Strategy and Tactics

In everyday life, people do not realize the difficulties of creating a sense of unity and identity in a society as complex and populated with as diverse groups as the Danish.

To succeed, considerable understanding of contemporary times as well as an ability to create an exciting and unifying attraction is required.

The royal family has long since been stripped of its hard power. Unlike her predecessors, Queen Margrethe can't employ soldiers to defeat the enemy, lock up her opponents in damp dungeons, or use fear as a means to tie the nation together. 'Soft power' is the only viable means

The Yellow Palace in Amaliegade, a stately eighteenth century edifice, is home to the Queen's Royal Household.

of the modern Court to maintain its position. Though well aware of this, the Queen and the royal family also rely on a small group of professional advisors. This select circle consists of Lord Chamberlain Ove Ullerup, Private Secretary Henning Fode and Communications and Press Secretary, Lene Balleby. They collaborate with the heads of the other Royal Households, including Chamberlain Christian Schønau, head of the Crown Prince's Secretariat at Amalienborg.

The Lord Chamberlain

Ove Ullerup is essential in exercising 'soft power'. The Lord Chamberlain is the supreme head of the Lord Chamberlain's Office, the largest part of the Court, and Ullerup is responsible for the cross-disciplinary coordination of the Court's overall tasks. In this capacity, he plays a crucial part in maintaining the force and magic of the royal family.

The Queen knows what her role as monarch involves—and what it does not involve—and she is able to balance the many conflicting demands of the royal family. She will, however, also draw on the Lord Chamberlain and his staff, who, in addition to running a spotless administration, must be aware of the latest trends and developments and uphold strong ties between the royal family and the world of arts, business and social institutions. The Lord Chamberlain's Office maintains relations with the politicians on Christiansborg, but it is also important that they have a well-operated royal house with responsible use of public funds.

In 2004, Ove Ullerup and financial manager Søren Weiskopf Kruse opened the books, making it easier to monitor how the royal family's funding is managed. The website of the Court (www.kongehuset.dk) has a detailed report on the royal family business. The next step will be to bring more clarity to the indirect support of the royal family. Internally, it is the view that the Danish royal family is operated in an efficient and cost-consciously manner, and presenting a proper financial report that includes all costs would be a logical next step. Presenting the total amount would, however, not be without risk. Summing up all contributions to the Court would obviously increase the final amount, which could draw criticism and make it seem that the royal family is swimming in money.

The response from the Court would be that, for example, the Royal Life Guards and the Royal Danish Hussar Guard Regiment have many functions besides being available to the royal family, and that the royal palaces are part of our heritage and need protection anyway. Should a majority at some point prefer to have a president as head of state, this would obviously also be costly. Heated media debates, however, tend to drown out all such arguments.

Lord Chamberlain Ove Ullerup addressing part of the staff at the Yellow Palace during preparations for the Queen's birthday.

Close Interaction

To ensure a consistent appearance of the royal house, the Lord Chamberlain maintains a close, internal dialogue between the various managers and small administrations. The most important advisors work closely together on certain cases, such as when the question of a new Act of Succession was raised, or when the Crown Prince expressed his wish to become a member of the IOC. Since such vital matters can affect the position of the entire Court, the counsellors will naturally align their assessments, agree on how to handle affairs and how to communicate to the surrounding world.

The Crown Prince's desire to join the IOC became what internally is called a 'house affair'. The Queen got involved, and the inner circle of advisors took part in the process from start to finish. The Crown Prince is presently a member of the IOC, and the matter is now in the hands of Chamberlain Christian Schønau at the Crown Prince's Secretariat. Should serious issues arise, more people will once again be summoned.

The senior managers of the royal house gather on a weekly basis with the Lord Chamberlain at the Yellow Palace to coordinate the activities of the royal family. Periodically, larger meetings will be held to plan, one year in advance, the tasks of the Royal Couple and the Crown Prince

Information meeting at the Yellow Palace.

Couple. The Lord Chamberlain's Office takes care of the overall setting of the Queen and the royal family; they make sure that events are planned down to the last detail and that the numbers are balanced. It is also part of the Lord Chamberlain's duties to act as a guard as well as a listening post for the Queen, and to ensure, aided by other counsellors, that the Court retains its relevance and its soft power.

For example; when planning a state visit to Korea, how do you convince a group of artists to join the royal family? Their participation cannot be taken for granted. When they do come along, it is not only that the Queen is the person she is and that they respect her cultural acumen, but also because the Court nurtures close alliances with the Ministry of Culture, The Danish Agency for Culture, and the artists themselves. Naturally, they also come along on the trip because they benefit professionally from doing so. Prosaic as it may sound, a modern royal family needs to provide added value, just like any other business. At the Russian state visit in April 2010, the Court aided in bringing together the leaders of the Danish corporate world and the Russian delegation. It is not enough for the royal family to merely collaborate with the Prime Minister's Office and the Ministry of Foreign Affairs about the state visit. The royal family must retain direct contact with key players of the corporate world.

Renewal

Most people are familiar with the pictures of court employees lining up, dressed in gala, at official events. But those photos are somewhat misleading, depicting the royal family's employees as if they lived at a distance from the real world. To perform their daily tasks, they very much need to keep their ears to the ground and know what is going on in society.

As would be the case in any other modern company, Ove Ullerup has implemented a process to define and map the objectives of the Court's administration. It took one year to formulate the goals, a process that involved the entire staff. External consultants were called in, somewhat to the chagrin of older employees who feared the consequences of opening up the royal family to outsiders. What if confidential information was leaked? Today, drawing on outside experts is more common, and it is generally more accepted when employees, after being affiliated with the royal family for a few years, move on to new challenges.

Contrary to what people might assume, adoring the royal family is not an essential quality. Quite the contrary. Good judgment and a critical mind are the best qualifications. If 'crazy about the royal family' is the primary incentive for seeking appointment at the Court, one will be met with misgivings.

Close to the Danes

The personal judgment of each member of the royal family is of the utmost importance. Despite leading very unusual lives, they have to be able to understand what happens in Denmark and among the Danes. Without this ability, the members of the royal family would be unable to respond appropriately to prevailing currents, and they would be ill-equipped to address one of the most difficult challenges of the time: The balance between accessibility and distance, between openness and dignity, between folksiness and distinction.

When the Queen approached her 70th birthday and preparations were about to commence, the advisors considered how to get the entire Danish population involved. Would it be best to rent Parken, Denmark's National Stadium with 40.000 seats? No, because no one could imagine the Queen in Parken. How about a gala at the Amalienborg Palace Square? No, because that could not include all Danes in the country. Finally, the Court entered into an agreement with the publicly owned television station TV2 about a live, prime time broadcast with two of Denmark's best-loved hosts, Jes Dorph-Petersen and Cecilie Frøkjær.

It was estimated that a very large part of the population had seen the broadcast. An appropriate balance between popular appeal and royal grandeur had also been kept, even if the boundaries were challenged by the comedian/magician Rune Klan's routine about 'the Queen Ham'. This involved the monarch initialising a small piece of paper, which was then clipped to a piece of ham. The ham embarked on a remarkable journey, first by disappearing, then by reappearing from out of one the entertainer's shoes, baked into a bun. The details of the trick are still being pondered.

Across the Nation

Naturally, a birthday celebration calls for extra consideration, but the task of ensuring the broad appeal of the royal family is systematically addressed at all times. It is carefully considered with whom the royal family will be meeting, to which places they will go, and which cruises the Dannebrog yacht will be taking. Prior to each visit, it will be discussed whether the focus should be on local businesses, schools, social institutions, or the local cultural centre. The Queen cares a great deal about these visits, and they almost never seem forced; the Queen and the other members of the royal family know how arrive in a natural way, be greeted by many people and, in each case, establish some sort of contact.

The mayors around the country are often the hosts when the royal family comes to visit, so for the Queen's birthday, all ninety-eight of them were invited to the party in Copenhagen. Much consideration is always given to how the royal family should form attachments—and with whom. The October concerts at Fredensborg Palace were held for years, and the invitees had traditionally been 'friends of the house', but then a consensus emerged to invite new groups of people, such as the Olympic team. These adjustments may appear less than revolutionary, yet they fortify the royal family's foundation and extricate the institution from old alliances. The royal family should not enjoy support from only a small and privileged part of the population. In a modern society, broad support is required.

The Private Secretary

The Private Secretary is the Queen's closest advisor when it comes to carrying out her constitutional duties. Henning Fode is the link between the regent and the political system: The parliament, the government and the ministries on Slotsholmen. He will continuously update the Queen on current affairs that she, once the minutes have been recorded, will discuss with the Prime Minister and the Minister of Foreign Affairs. These two ministers will, unless prevented by travel, meet with the Queen at Amalienborg every other Wednesday. The Prime Minister arrives at 11 o'clock, and a meeting regarding domestic politics typically lasts about half an hour. Then the Minister of Foreign Affairs reports on world affairs. The Queen is alone with the ministers during these talks. No public servants participate in the confidential meetings.

The Private Secretary will also advise the Queen regarding requests for patronage as well as invitations to participate in smaller or larger events. State visits belong to the latter category, and the Lord Chamberlain and the Private Secretary are both deeply involved in planning the Queen's travels abroad or visits from foreign heads of state. All state visits are discussed and planned by a special committee with the participation of top advisors from the Court and public servants from the Prime Minister's Office and the Ministry of Foreign Affairs. Many considerations are made: Which international relations should Denmark strengthen? Which industrial policies and commercial interests are at play? A decision will eventually be made by

the Queen, her closest advisors, the Private Secretary and Lord Chamberlain, and the two ministries involved.

The planning of large ceremonial events such as state visits are assigned to the Lord Chamberlain's Office, and yet another key adviser, the Master of Ceremonies Christian Eugen-Olsen, will join the group. Prior to the visits, the Private Secretary will ensure that the wording of the regent's official speeches correspond with official Danish policy.

The Council of State

During the Folketing session from October to June, the Private Secretary keeps track of the paper flow coming from the lawmakers in the ministries on Slotsholmen. He also has a central role in preparing the meetings of the Council of State. Historically, the Council of State was held once a week. At the meeting, the ministers would request the King's permission to propose new legislation and have the majesty sign laws that were already adopted. Today, the series of meetings are more flexible. Extensive travelling by the head of government, not the least due to meetings in the EU, makes regular meetings of the Council of State difficult to plan. The Council of State will normally be held eight or nine times during a Folketing session, and all ministers aim to be present around the large conference table, where considerable amounts of papers are moved back and forth between the ministers and the Queen. The Council of State may have seventy-eight laws on the agenda, all of which must physically be signed and ratified by the Queen.

The Council of State has formal and concise procedures. If the Minister of Foreign Affairs has a case, the minister will rise and say what needs to be done with the bill on the Queen's table. When the Queen has signed the paper, the case is handed back to the minister.

New Government

All of this is fairly predictable and uneventful, though avoiding errors is obviously important. The real test of a Private Secretary, however, takes place under completely different and more unpredictable conditions. The Private Secretary is the Queen's principal advisor when a new government is being formed, and both regent and advisor are in close proximity when the power is placed. The process normally proceeds in an orderly manner. The Prime Minister will go to the Queen the day after a general election to brief her on the result and inform her about the Prime Minister's own conclusions. The Queen will record if the government has the necessary majority to continue. That, in principle, is it. If, however, there is ambiguity as to how a government can be formed, a far more complicated process will begin. The Private Secretary will then discuss with the permanent secretary for the Prime Minister what the minister intends to say to the Queen. The Prime Minister will most likely announce that the election results not unequivocally indicate that he can continue. He will then recommend the Queen summon the representatives of the parties to hear their views on the formation of a new government.

The Private Secretary will call the Prime Minister and announce that the Queen intends to summon the representatives of each political party to Amalienborg. The party leaders, arriving according to the size of their party, will hand two copies of their advice, in writing, to the Queen. These will then be analyzed at Amalienborg and at the Prime Minister's Office. When the permanent secretary for the Prime Minister and the Private Secretary agree on the conclusion, the Private Secretary will go to the Queen. Frequently, a chief negotiator will be appointed, and in more complicated cases several rounds and exploratory talks are needed before a government can be formed.

The Queen meets with the Prime Minister and each of the party leaders alone, but the Private Secretary knows exactly what has been said as they hand over their advice in writing and in duplicate. This process can, in other words, be documented and verified.

Balancing Act

The Queen is not allowed to make political decisions, but there are historical examples of the monarch performing a difficult balancing act. In January 1993, Prime Minister Poul Schlüter of the Conservative Party was forced to leave office after the publication of the report on the so-called 'Tamil affair'. The possibility of letting his government continue with a new head of government was considered. However, by intervention of the Queen's Private Secretary, Niels Eilschou-Holm, Poul Schlüter decided to call off this venture. Political scientists and experts on constitutional law have since scrutinized the process. Some have compared it with the situation in 1962 when the ailing Prime Minister Viggo Kampmann from his hospital bed handed over the power to Jens Otto Krag. Others have pointed out that Jens Otto Krag later handed Anker Jørgensen the keys to the Prime Minister's Office. However, no strict parallel can be drawn between Poul Schlüter and his two predecessors, as Schlüter's government in 1993 no longer had an intact majority. The Social-Liberal Party had withdrawn their support. During this tense drama, the Queen and the Private Secretary's Office were directly involved in the political process. Dramatic and exciting as it may sound, the situation was less than desirable. It is much preferred that the politicians know and play by the rules.

Other prime ministers have been replaced with much less drama. In 2009, after being confirmed as the NATO Secretary General, Anders Fogh Rasmussen went to the Queen to inform her about his coming resignation and to request that the Queen appoint Lars Løkke Rasmussen as the new Prime Minister. Following that, the Private Secretary asked Løkke—formally—if he was willing to undertake the task, and he was then asked to come see the Queen and take on the duties of head of government.

The process may sound unnecessarily complicated, but the formal approach ensures a transformation of power that is in accordance with the provisions of the constitution. Absolute clarity is essential, and everything must be executed with the utmost care.

The Welcome

The newly appointed head of government or the newly formed government are presented to the public at the Amalienborg Palace Square, accompanied by hoorays and congratulating fellow party members amid a swarm of reporters and news photographers. Prior to this, the government has met with the Queen inside the palace. The ministers arrive at Amalienborg in ministerial cars, and the prime minister introduces them, according to their rank, to the Queen and the Crown Prince. The Queen expresses her joy at meeting the ministers and then wishes them good luck. She is careful not to make any political statements. Whatever her likes and dislikes, she keeps them to herself, and the colour of the new government, whether red or blue, never affects her friendly and encouraging greeting.

The ministers are served champagne and cake, and the Prime Minister improvises a short speech before everyone walks into the palace square. In a government reshuffle, the Queen welcomes the new ministers before they enter the palace square. Shortly thereafter, the outgoing ministers arrive in an entirely different mood. Though a few may be relieved that the workload has been lifted from their shoulders, most are unhappy or even bitter. The Queen greets them individually, thanking them for their effort.

The Pressure of the Press

The royal family has in recent years become more accessible to the press, and since the press creates the image that most Danes have of the royal family, they also influence how soft power works. When Ove Ullerup headhunted former head of TV-Avisen, Lis M. Frederiksen, and made her the Court's first public relations officer, it was a step toward professionalizing media relations. Internally, it stirred outrage. Some found it frivolous of the royal family to have information managers, while others feared they would now engage in the same kind of spin and manipulation as some of the more infamous Christiansborg spin-doctors. Nonetheless, it soon became clear that the new public relations officer filled a need. Later, Lene Balleby was hired as Communications and Press Secretary, and she has further professionalized the royal family's communication. This is not a Danish phenomenon. Across Europe, the royal houses prepare to meet the challenges from the media. The very traditional British royal house employs a large group of experts who work with new ways of communicating. By establishing The Royal Channel—the official online channel of the British Monarchy—the aging Queen Mother now has a presence on the newest media platform.

It would be unrealistic for the Danish royal family to use the same amount of resources, but Amalienborg does pay attention to how other royal houses adapt. The top administrative leaders will from time to time gather at international meetings, and the communications advisors remain in contact across borders.

The accelerated pace of the media represents a mutual challenge. Web sites have a constant news flow and stories make their way across cyberspace in no time. The heavy media exposure is at the same time a privilege and a burden to the royal family. In the eyes of the Court, it is important that the royals are visible and that people pay attention to them. An invisible royal family is not a powerful royal family, and lacking exposure would undermine the institution's relevance in the minds of people. The stories in the weekly magazines play their part in making the royals relevant. Several magazines have reporters who specialize in the royal family and know what is going on at Amalienborg.

The real problem for the royal family is a certain form of "journalism" that would never be acceptable in the traditional media. The practitioners violate the boundaries of the private sphere and will invent a story based on a single photo. This is one of the major challenges of Lene Balleby and her international colleagues: Battling the media's tendency to move from the official sphere to the private sphere. "The extensive publicity would not be a problem if the stories originated in the official activities and tasks of the royal family. The problem arises the moment focus is moved from cause to person, from official life to private life," says Lene Balleby.

Focus Areas

As a counterbalance, the members of the royal family will focus on very specific tasks and emphasize that being royal means performing a function. Crown Princess Mary's focus is the fight against social isolation. She has talked about violence against women and has increased the awareness of bullying among children. Crown Prince Fre-

derik joined the IOC in an effort to advocate sports and illuminate the connection between exercise and public health. The favourite causes of Norway's Crown Prince Haakon include climate change, a focus he shares with Crown Prince Frederik and Sweden's Crown Princess Victoria. The three heirs to the throne travelled to Svalbard and Greenland to study the effects of climate change in the Arctic region, and their participation in other inter-Scandinavian campaigns, such as a panel discussion at the 2009 Climate Summit, has attracted much attention from Danish and international media.

Public duties aside, the royals must also be careful in their spare time. The weekly magazines will, quite literally, equate them with sports and rock stars or well-know people from popular TV shows. Too close an association with the jetset or celebrity universe could reduce any royal to being merely famous and eventually put the institution at risk. In short: Noblesse oblige.

Necessary Boundaries

The Court counsellors work to secure a certain amount of personal space for the royal family, and not just behind closed doors at Amalienborg. The hunting property called "Trend" in the woods of northern Jutland is one of few places where the royals are left completely alone. In all other places, the public can potentially get within a radius of a few meters, and modern technology has only made the circle smaller. But if they royals were to be constantly monitored, they would not be able to live as human beings. Should the Court attempt to set up boundaries, certain news editors might begin to talk about a violation of the freedom of speech. The royal family would reply, however, that it is not about free speech. "It's about curiosity and a level of intrusion that no other people would or should accept," says Ove Ullerup. The Lord Chamberlain dismisses the premise that since the royals receive appanage from the state, they simply have to live with it. He warns that this kind of reasoning could lead to the royals being pursued and monitored round the clock.

Confrontations so far have been few, partly because no Danish media can compete with the ruthlessness of the media in other countries, and partly because of the Danish tradition of consensus. For this reason, the royal family refrains from involving lawyers or lodging complaints to the Press Council even if groundless stories are printed. Only in the event of serious misrepresentation of facts will a call be made to the journalists and editors.

Amalienborg keeps a close watch on developments in the media at home and abroad. In Britain, the Queen has approached newspaper and magazine editors to ask that the media show more respect. In Holland, a media code exists between the Court and the press, and the Dutch crown prince couple will press charges against those who invade their privacy. In other countries, the royal families have their own lawyers, and written codes regulate what the press can do when covering the royals. It was noted at Amalienborg when Princess Caroline of Monaco won a case and was awarded compensation by the International Court of Justice. The ruling did not outlaw photographing the royals, but it did set certain boundaries. While these things are seen as small victories, no one has any illusions. None of the closest advisors believe that privacy will again be granted to the members of the royal family.

Next in Line

The Queen is the present monarch, and while all of her advisors naturally assist her as best as possible, everyone knows that a generational handover of the Crown is moving closer, and they work to prepare the Crown Prince and the Crown Princess for the task. The Crown Prince is being introduced to the basic tasks, such as the Council of the State, state visits and touring the country to meet the people. They also work on making the Crown Prince more comfortable when delivering speeches to large groups and to the media. Though Crown Prince Frederik has been extremely popular for years, he has often faltered when he had to address large gatherings or appear on television.

However, at the Queen's 70th birthday, facing a distinguished group of royalty from across Europe and an entire nation watching on live television, he delivered a precise, comprehensive and personal speech. The family as well as the Court were relieved that he did this so convincingly. It proved that practice indeed makes perfect. Part of the preparations deal with navigating an era of heavy media pressure where the mood might suddenly change.

Historically, the royal family has always had the ability to fashion individuals who were adept at manifesting their own style in relation to their times. This could be said for

King Frederik IX and Queen Margrethe, and for Crown Prince Frederik who by demonstrating the same ability has endeared himself to a large part of the population. The Court is profoundly confident that the Crown Prince will become a competent regent, but they are also aware that he will carry this out in different ways than the Queen. Monarchs are given no scripts and must shape the role they will be playing, but it pays to be prepared, and for the Crown Prince, preparations have already begun.

In the Crown Prince's struggle to become a member of the IOC, it was all but overlooked that this was a chance for him to learn the diplomatic craft, an experience that is difficult for an heir to the throne to acquire before ascending to the Crown. At the same time he signalled to the public, as the Queen has previously done, that though the royals are well aware of the limitations of their position, they will not let themselves be reduced to playing parts in a comic-opera court.

The Lord Chamberlain

From a military man to a diplomat. That was more or less the situation in 2003 when Ove Ullerup replaced Søren Haslund-Christensen as the Queen's Lord Chamberlain. After serving as Ambassador to Vietnam, Ove Ullerup returned to the Danish Ministry of Foreign Affairs to serve as Under-Secretary for Multilateral Affairs. He had previously been stationed in Bangkok for UNHCR and had been a delegate of the Ministry of Foreign Affairs at the Danish UN mission in New York and at the EU Representation in Brussels.

A diplomat all the way, Ove Ullerup has a distinct ability to make contacts and is used to analysing developments in world affairs. In his approach to the task as Lord Chamberlain, Ove Ullerup resembles the former Director General of Danmarks Radio, Hans Sølvhøj, who also became the Queen's Lord Chamberlain. Both have a pronounced ability to read the signs of their time and adapt the Court to the changes. Internally, Ullerup has helped modernise the Royal Household's administra-

tion; externally he has strengthened the relationship of the Court with the outside world.

Formally, the Lord Chamberlain is the Chief Administrative Officer of the Royal Household. The Lord Chamberlain's Office is located at the Yellow Palace in Amaliegade, and its duties include managing economy, foundations

and communications. From days of old, the term 'Court' has been used for the Royal Family's household and administration. Some 130 employees are divided into a number of small administrations, called Royal Households. The members of the Royal House each have their own small administration.

THE PRIVATE SECRETARY

In August 2007, Henning Fode became the new Private Secretary to the Queen, and his appointment followed a tradition of recruiting an outstanding attorney. His predecessor, Niels Eilschou Holm, was also known for his extensive legal knowledge, and this particular skill—combined with the ability to keep a cool, analytical head under pressure, e.g. under a government formation—is crucial to the job.

From the position of Public Prosecutor, Henning Fode came to Amalienborg to head the Private Secretary's Office. It is his primary task to assist the regent in carrying out her duties as defined by the Danish constitution. Once the process of forming a new government comes to an end, the Private Secretary will prepare the Council of State where the laws of the country will receive Royal Assent. It's also part of his job to give advice in connection with numerous inquiries from organizations, businesses and institutions requesting a visit by the Queen. Along with the Lord Chamberlain, the Private Secretary advises on decisions regarding state visits and he will also assist in the preparation of official speeches.

In his capacity as chief of the Chapter of the Royal Orders of Chivalry, Henning Fode will present recipients nominated for orders. A large part of the orders are given to someone who is stepping up the career ladder, for example when an officer advances in the hierarchy at the Castle Islet (Slotsholmen, the location of the seat of the Danish Parliament), but orders are also given to others as an appreciation of their work.

THE COMMUNICATIONS AND PRESS SECRETARY

In January 2008, Lene Balleby took over the responsibility of the Royal Household's communication after Lis M. Frederiksen, the Court's first press officer. In addition to being the Minister Counsellor (Press & Cultural Affairs) at the Embassy of Denmark in Washington D.C., Lene Balleby worked a number of years as Director of Communications at Egmont. She has first hand knowledge of the media world she works with and struggles against within her role as primary media advisor to the royal family.

Lene Balleby works for the royal family on several levels. She is responsible for the development of the internal and external communications of the house. She is a member of the management group at the Yellow Palace, and she will, on a more general level, advise on strategic positioning of the royal family in the media. She is also involved when magazines, newspapers, broadcasting companies and publishers submit specific proposals for interviews, transmissions, movies and books about the royals.

The tougher part of the job involves shielding the royal family when the media, in the eyes of the Court, becomes too intrusive. She has on several occasions acted as spokesman, for instance when massive and totally erroneous rumours had it that the Queen intended to abdicate. Though Lene Balleby works across all Royal Households and will advise all members of the royal family, she primarily works for the Queen, the Prince Consort, and for the Crown Prince and Crown Princess.

THE CHAMBERLAIN

Crown Prince Frederik and Crown Princess Mary have their own Royal Household at Frederik VIII's Palace. This independent organization, consisting of about twenty-five people with different functions, will solve all tasks associated with the daily activities of the Crown Prince Couple. Former Permanent Secretary, Christian Schønau, who carries the title of Chamberlain, heads the organization. This is a completely independent unit that will collaborate with the Queen's Royal Household at the Yellow Palace. The two Households have a weekly coordination meeting on Tuesday mornings where they brief each other on the upcoming tasks of the Queen and Crown Prince, and, if necessary, arrange ad hoc meetings. Although the Crown Prince and the Queen usu-ally have different tasks and activities, coordination is still needed.

Chamberlain Christian Schønau, who has a Master of Law degree, had a meteoric career with the Government Departments, so the public was surprised when the person who had once been the country's youngest Permanent Secretary—first at the Ministry of the Interior and Health, then at the new Ministry of Health, and finally at the Ministry of Social Affairs—could suddenly be found in an entirely different world, far away from the political conflicts of the Castle Islet (Slotsholmen). Christian Schønau succeeded Chamberlain Per Thornit, a close associate of the Crown Prince for many years, when he retired in 2010. The position of Chamberlain is not advertised. The royal family hand-picked the new Chamberlain with the assistance of professional consultants.

In recent yeas, the Crown Prince Couple have increasingly taken over representative task from the Queen, especially those of a cultural and, especially, commercial nature. The Crown Prince is often requested to represent the nation as the head of Danish business delegations abroad, a task the Court willingly assumes when given the opportunity. On these trips, Christian Schønau usually comes along, just as he plays a pivotal role in planning most other of the Crown Prince's activities, aside from his sporting interests and his involvement with the International Olympic Committee. Private Secretary, Morten Roland-Hansen, is the Crown Prince's closest adviser in those areas.

The Chamberlain Christian Schønau with Morten Roland Hansen (left).

Surrounded by Friendly Ghosts

Interview with the Crown Prince

Crown Prince Frederik has on two occasions lived in the same buildings and same rooms as Queen Ingrid, who played a crucial role early on in his life. Thinking back on his Amalienborg childhood, the most memorable moments were not the pomp and circumstance of official events, quite the opposite. It was when his grandmother—Queen Ingrid—invited her two grandchildren, Crown Prince Frederik and Prince Joachim for tea in Frederik VIII's Palace where she resided in winter, from early November to late March. "These visits always had a warmth and cosiness about them. It was the dark time of the year and we would gather in the room with the fireplace," recalls the Crown Prince. At this time, Queen Ingrid occupied only a small part of the palace.

The ground floor was closed off when she became dowager queen after the death of King Frederik IX in January of 1972. The banquet hall was rarely used, but when it did happen, it was a celebration. "Grandmother would on several occasions host a party for me and my cousins. There were six of us who were about the same age. And when we to this day remain more than just distant cousins, it's because of her efforts to gather us around her. And we did get along well with each other."

When the cousins from abroad came to visit, they darted around the great halls at "full throttle", as the Crown Prince's puts it. King Konstantin and Queen Anne-Marie and their children stayed with Queen Ingrid for a while, until they moved to London in the early 1970s. As often as Frederik and Joachim could get away with it, they would go to the palace and play hide and seek in the large build-

ing. In the fantasy world of a child, the dark green staircase seemed scary and menacing, but apart from that grandma's palace was synonymous with warmth and good atmosphere. "She had all these amazing things in her rooms—interesting furniture, porcelain figurines, and lots of knick-knacks. Some of this she had inherited from her mother, who came from England, other things came from her childhood home in Sweden. It was a home with history, style, calm, balance and hygge. Even as a kid, one could sense these things. It was always pleasant to visit her."

The Central Person

Queen Ingrid was the person that the Crown Prince and his generation of princes and princesses gathered around, and he recalls how she would always be a part of the young people's lived. "She paid attention to all of us, but of course especially her own two Danish grandchildren who also geographically were closer. Due to the order of succession, I might have occupied a special place in her universe, and though she never pointed this out, it was implicit in her care. She had a certain ability to never mention this topic directly, but it was always clear that she was interested. She was always there."

As the Crown Prince grew older, the visits became less frequent and Queen Ingrid would instead call to ask how things were. "It was very considerate of her, and she seemed more aware of our doings than we perhaps realized." Queen Ingrid was also the Crown Prince's confidante. "I would ask her other questions than I would ask my parents, which I recall as a huge privilege. Back in the day, older generations were generally regarded as worldly-wise or having gained a special wisdom. She fully possessed this wisdom until the end of her life, and that's how we all saw her, not just my cousins and I, but probably also my mom and her sisters." The Crown Prince grew up with Queen Ingrid at his side, a wise Queen who was a grandmother as well as an advisor to her grandchild, who in his younger years at times felt uncomfortable in the position of heir to the throne. "I see her as my mentor—someone who doesn't agree with you on everything, someone who will work with you and your questions and make you think in such ways as to find the answer. It's a teacher in the Buddhist tradition, a person who will guide you on the way."

Grandfather's Sabre

One event in particular epitomises how the Crown Prince overcame his crisis and made the successful transition from an insecure adolescent to a confident heir to the throne, and from somewhat lost teenager to a dynamic officer. The event took place after his completion of several demanding and gruelling military trainings, and at the time when received his MSc degree in political science "She lived to see me complete my education, and she witnessed my Army and Navy careers. My grandfather had been a seaman to the core, so it made her proud that I had also chosen that path. When I began—and finished—my

frogman core training it added an extra dimension and meant something special." When the Crown Prince was appointed naval officer, he was called to see Queen Ingrid. The year was 1995 and he wore his new uniform. "I was dressed to the nines. I went up the stairs and entered the room. My grandmother waited inside with my parents and several officers from my unit. This was where she handed me my grandfather's sabre, given to him when he became a naval officer. It was a big moment for me—and for grandma."

The old Queen herself, bowed with age, walked to the Crown Prince and handed him the sabre. Everyone knew this was a special moment: Pingo—as the Crown Prince was called—had overcome the challenges. He had shown courage and strength. And he had passed. Now he could carry the sabre that had at one time been carried by his grandfather the seaman, sailor, and King.

Palace Childhood

In the years leading up to this transitional moment with Queen Ingrid, the Crown Prince had his childhood at a Amalienborg, a childhood that most children would probably not recognise; yet there was room for them to be children. The boy's domain was the small nursery and classroom that had been set up in Christian VII's Palace in the years 1971-75. "It wasn't exactly a padded cell, but it was a suitable space for two boys. Fortunately, there were no chandeliers or expensive wallpaper that could be damaged."

The two brothers played football in the hallways of the Palace attic. Sometimes aides or police officers would act as playmates, and then they would all play cops and robbers. Fredensborg Palace with its gardens, forest and lake did, however, surpass Amalienborg when it came to playing wild games. The boys turned the long, interior hallways of Fredensborg into football fields and shooting galleries. "In those days, the hallways had no runners and no hanging lamps, only these dull, crescent-shaped, UFO-like lamps that shone on the ceiling with a dim light. Nor was there any of the present day antlers hanging on the walls. And in these hallways we kicked the football back and forth."

At one time, a nanny came to check up on the boys just as the ball had been kicked with a clean instep kick. The Crown Prince alternates between playfulness and guilt when he recalls how the ball struck the stunned nanny. On another occasion the princes hit the ceiling lights, an incident that was not applauded.

People waiting in line to visit the totally refurbished Frederik VIII's Palace are in for a surprise when the future occupant of the palace comes walking by.

Different Times

In the city, the two brothers wreaked havoc in the attic of Amalienborg, a place that the Crown Price has dubbed the "cylinder head". It was not a bad childhood, even if the two boys, compared to their peers outside the palace walls, lived at a greater distance to their parents. "It was all right and it never bothered us," says the Crown Prince. "The times were different, and it never seemed unnatural to us, though obviously it didn't allow for the same intimacy as we now share with our children. Palaces and castles are large buildings with large distances. My parents could of course have fitted a playroom into the palace where they lived, but they wanted the palace to remain as originally intended, so we had our rooms up there, and it was fine."

The Crown Prince, however, doesn't intend for his own children to grow up with the same distance, and though he previously has spoken critically about his childhood, he is now careful not to blame his parents. Likewise, he distances himself from accounts stating that his childhood was marked by isolation and loneliness. "In the fairy tales the King always has an unhappy life at the palace. Or we hear tales about a princess without her prince, and vice versa. They're all lonely, unhappy and without companions. But my brother and I were not lonely. We had our parents and we had each other." He and his brother once revealed in a speech that they were four years old before they had dinner with their parents, and it caused a storm of indignation, but the Crown Prince has since made it clear that this arrangement seemed natural to them. They had never lived any other way.

"Had it been a bad experience, we probably wouldn't have talked about it," he later said in an interview with Berlingske Tidende. The two princes had friends and playmates, and though circumstances were different, there was room to play. "We couldn't walk with our friends to school, or go home with them after school, but occasionally we did have friends come over to our house after school or on weekends. If you ask them, they'll probably say it was exciting to be here, and they handled it well. They were our friends and we played as kids do. We roamed around and played football in the garden."

As an adolescent, the Crown Prince felt burdened by the restrictions to his life. "In high school, I thought that it was downright mean that I had to sit there and listen to my friends telling stories on Monday morning about their first trip to town. When they spoke about all the things they had experienced Friday and Saturday night, all one could do was sit there and think, "Why can't I do that?" My brother and I had to go home, and sometimes it seemed so much more limited. On the other hand, I realize it wasn't justifiable if we swept around town. We were underage, and people knew who we were, so we couldn't just say we'd drink only a glass of water or milk when we headed to town."

Maturation

In 1982, the two brothers were sent to the Ecole des Roches boarding school in Normandy, France, which was not a very memorable period. The Crown Prince was only 13 years old when he and his younger brother Joachim arrived at this strange elite school, the name of which translates to 'The school on the rocks.' And these French rocks turned out to be a painful experience.

He has since revealed that he never felt as lost as when he saw his parents' car drive away, and the transition to the firm schooling was tough. Their upbringing at home had also been very resolute: "When the court had ruled, there was nothing to do (...) You could cry behind closed doors or be furious, but it was not open for discussion." Years later, the Crown Prince was criticized for being a party prince who was too preoccupied with girls, fast cars and partying with the jetset to take his role as heir to the throne seriously. At several official events the Crown Prince appeared to be uncomfortable with the focus on his person. Though the parents sheltered their boys from the public, more serious words might have been spoken in private—and all the while the parents tried to give their sons room to be young and become adults. Christian VIII's palace was furnished with an apartment and reception rooms for the Crown Prince, so that he could "leave home". And it was while he kept himself somewhat out of the public eye that the Crown Prince gradually began to accept his destiny. He grew, developed his skills, and educated himself with more and more determination.

Graduate and Soldier

After graduating from Øregaard Gymnasium in 1986 he studied political science and economics at the University of Aarhus and received his MSc in 1995. He also studied

one year at Harvard University, and worked three months at the Danish UN mission in New York as part of his schooling in international politics. From October 1998 to October 1999 he was posted as First Secretary at the Danish Embassy in Paris.

Though these experiences alone constituted a solid foundation, the training and education in the armed forces undoubtedly contributed most to the Crown Prince's transformation. His perhaps most significant trial was the rigorous frogman training, a program that few have the stamina to complete. But the Crown Prince's military career begins long before that. In 1986, he was enrolled as a private in the Royal Life Guards. He was appointed lieutenant of the reserve in 1988, and subsequently served as platoon commander in the Royal Danish Hussar Guard Regiment. The following year he was appointed first lieutenant of the reserve (army).

In 1995, he was appointed first lieutenant of the reserve (navy), and from there he rose through the ranks. From 2001 to 2002, he completed further training for leaders at the Royal Danish Defence College. Next year he served as staff officer at Defence Command Denmark, and from 2003 he was a senior lecturer with the Institute of Strategy at the Royal Defence College. In other words, the Crown Price has learned the demanding craft of an elite soldier and has given lectures on military strategy. In addition to using his physique as a soldier, he has participated in demanding expeditions, not least with 'Expedition Sirius 2000', a four-month and 2.795 km long dog-sledge expedition around the northern tip of Greenland during extreme weather conditions. In his diary from the trip, he tells about waking in the morning to crawl out and brush snow off of the tent, and in an instant go from plus thirty to minus thirty degrees centigrade.

On this journey he became more and more fascinated with Greenland, and Danes have since witnessed how special the island and the Greenlanders are to the Crown Prince. Danish television broadcast the Crown Prince's return to one of the distant villages he had previously visited and the overwhelming welcome he received. Since his days in the frogman corps, he has kept up the hard physical training, and he is undoubtedly one of the fittest members of Europe's royal families, a man who rides horseback, plays tennis, runs, rides mountain bikes and participates in boat races at an international level.

Mary

Most important of all, however, was meeting a certain Mary Elizabeth Donaldson. The wedding ceremony took place on May 14, 2004, at the Church of Our Lady (the national cathedral of Denmark), where the Australian girl became H.R.H. Crown Princess Mary of Denmark. The Crown Prince's joy of being united with the woman he loved overshadowed all the new and distinguished titles and privileges. The whole nation witnessed on live television the happiness of the Crown as he watched his future wife walk down the aisle. Prince Christian was born in October 2005, Princess Isabella in April 2007, and it's not a secret how much the Crown Prince loves being a father.

Detail of Jesper Christiansen's vestibule painting "Verdensrummet"
(The Space). Across continents and countries, peculiar details refer
to the private life of the Crown Prince Couple.

The Former Boy

This transformation was a central theme in a larger portrait book called "Frederik— Crown Prince of Denmark", published in connection with his 40th birthday on May 26, 2008. In a review in Politiken—aptly titled "The former boy"—the historian Jes Fabricius Møller called attention to two of the photos in the book. Both photos show the Crown Prince seated on a step at Amalienborg Palace. While the picture from 1970 depicts a lost boy, the one from 2008 shows a mature and serene man. The review in Kristeligt Dagblad mentioned the same formidable developmental history. The last lines of the review call the book "a comprehensive portrait confirming the assumption of a thoroughly likeable modern man." Also, one might add, a man with a certain edge, as the Crown Prince in recent years has gone far up the field in his desire to deal with things of substance.

Not a 'Coach Figure'

He says in the book that he doesn't want to be just a symbol—or a "coach figure". Though royal, he won't settle for cutting tape and waving from the balcony on birthdays. Those things are part of the job, and though aware of the limits, he insists on the freedom to choose the tasks that he finds of special importance and where he can make a difference. When the Crown Prince ran for the board of the IOC, his wish to take on new tasks became highly exposed, triggering fierce debate and criticism from press and policy makers alike.

Many critics felt that he had unambiguously crossed the boundaries of politics, and most newspaper editorials warned him against embarking on this venture. But he did not back out, though evidently he had made the central authorities and the Court both uneasy and concerned. He persisted in pursuing his possibilities of being elected so he could use his IOC membership as a platform to promote sports and focus on exercise as a way to improve public health. Though the project was risky and threatened to capsize, he saw it through.

Prior to the Copenhagen climate summit in December 2009, he assumed a more visible role by being one of the young royals warning against the consequences of climate change. He has created his own position step by step and mentioned the transformation in an interview a few years ago: "I have, by being myself, come further than I thought possible. Some might have thought that I had become a different person, but I can only say: What you see is what you get."

New Interactions with the Queen

The Crown Prince prepares himself for the day when he must take the lead. He tries to spend his time the right way and feels that each year he becomes better and better prepared for the monumental task of succeeding his mother, the Queen, and follow in her footsteps. In recent years, the two of them have interacted more and more closely, and if the Queen at times was distant and absent while the Crown Prince was a boy, they have in adult life

moved closer to each other and share each other's confidence. "These days we talk with each other in a totally different way, which of course also has something to do with the fact that my foundation has improved over the last ten to fifteen years. Now I dare to move closer."

That he is proud of his mother was emphasized in the speech he delivered at the Queen's 70th birthday celebration at Fredensborg Palace. In a speech that was televised live nationwide, the Crown Prince opened by saying that he had always felt safe with his mom: "In my early memories, being child and your son, was associated with the feeling of running through the house at Fredensborg, turning left at Red Salon, and then to sprint through Yellow Salon to your drawing room and into your arms." He mentioned how his mother had read aloud from The Lord of the Rings. No less than three times in five years were the two princes drawn into Tolkien's adventures universe about the fight between good and evil, with the Queen adding to the scenes by painting and drawing them on paper.

All was well until suddenly he "fell out of the fairy tale" when it dawned on him that he couldn't confine himself to being his mother's son. He was also the son of the Queen and would one day be the King of Denmark. Then came the struggle to catch up with the situation—by studying and exercising—and he recalled how the Queen rooted for him in a running competition in the woods south of Aarhus. Finally, he expressed gratitude and joy at witnessing the Queen's support of Crown Princess Mary, and he expressed delight at their ability to counsel each other. The exit was: "Dear Mother, you appear just like the

mother your two sons remember from their youth—a beautiful Queen, a doughty girl."

No sooner had he seated himself before the Crown Princess rushed over to give him a kiss. The speech, however, had not only moved his wife. In the Queen's own speech, she described her son's development in the ten years that had passed since her 60th birthday where Frederik had been in Greenland with The Sirius Patrol: "Now, here you are, a joyful, a more mature and a happy man with your own family. In the ten years that have passed, each year has brought us closer together. As Crown Prince, you support me well, and you are someone that I can talk to about everything."

Earlier that day, the Crown Prince along with the immediate family had accompanied the Queen on the balcony of Amalienborg Palace. Overlooking the crowded square it was hard for the Crown Prince not to notice the tremendous support his mother received and her important position in Danish society. "It was so heartfelt and gave me a lump in my throat. It's an amazing thing for us all to be greeted by so many people who wish to congratulate the Queen on her birthday and let her know that she is central to this fantastic image of Denmark that we share—one of the many good images."

The Houses of Queen Ingrid

The transformation of the Crown Prince from shy teenager to a powerful personality is also evident at the Amalienborg Palace where Queen Ingrid's old palace has also been transformed. As fate would have it, the Crown Prince has on two occasions moved into the fine homes of his beloved mentor. The first time was when he moved into the Kancellihuset (Chancellor's House) next to Fredensborg Palace, where Queen Ingrid lived for most of her final years. The Crown Prince and Crown Princess lived here for six full years, summer and winter, right until the palace at Amalienborg could be taken in possession.

The Crown Prince finds it natural to live in the same houses as his grandmother. "My family is blessed to be able to live in the buildings where our ancestors lived. My grandmother passed away peacefully in the very room of the Kancellihuset that is now our bedroom. I had to think about that at first, but there is a great spirit in the house. Sometimes a faint smell of cigarette smoke, spiced with perfumes will suddenly appear, and that's how we are reminded that grandma used to live here. There's nothing to be afraid of. One life has ended and new ones have begun, and our kids roam around and have fun in her old rooms."

A Tired House

The Crown Prince is very happy to take over the palace where Queen Ingrid and King Frederik lived and where his mother spent her childhood and adolescence along with her sisters, Princess Benedikte and Princess Anne-Marie. After one of the boldest restorations in history, the house now sparkles like a jewel. Five years passed before the palace in the spring of 2010 was opened for the press and public for a few months and almost half a million Danes waited patiently in line to see it. Once inside, they could admire the halls on the ground floor and the beletage—the two main floors of the palace that the Crown Prince will use for representational purposes. The visitors witnessed how the elegant late French empire style interiors, the nineteenth century ceilings, and the walls and mirrors all displayed works of art by Olafur Eliasson, Signe Guttormsen, Morten Schelde, John Kørner, Eske Kath, Kathrine Ærtebjerg, Kasper Bonnén, Tal R, Erik A. Frandsen, and Jesper Christiansen. It took the Crown Prince some time getting used to the idea of such a radical refurbishment and such dramatic changes to Queen Ingrid's old rooms. He often wondered if the renovations would be too extensive.

"The first few times we walked around inside the palace, before all the craftsmen arrived and demolition began, and I listened to the palace architect explaining the visions of the reconstruction, I thought to myself: "This is not going to work! It will be too open, too barren, too desolate." Obviously, the memories of grandma's home were still very present in my mind. When I thought about the fireplace where we had sat together so often, I found it difficult to visualize the room opened up and a double-leaf door installed."

However, the Crown Prince realized that the old palace

was in need of refurbishment. "I have visited many old houses and palaces while they were under construction, so I'm aware of the soul and spirit of these houses, and while this house obviously had a good spirit and soul, it was also a tired, slightly stooping house. When the house was all but stripped of its clothes and the builders began, that's when it became emotionally hard. By the fall of 2006, demolition had reached the last stage, everything had been torn down, and you couldn't get any further. This marked a kind of low end of a spiritual process, but moving forward, you could see that the mood of the palace rose. And since then it's been amazing to witness the development of the palace and how it radiates joy. It may sound far-fetched, but you can really feel the spirit of the house."

The Crown Prince discovered along the way that his wife had the same sensitivity toward old houses. She grew up in a single-family house and lived there with her parents and four siblings, but she could sense the spirit of Queen Ingrid's house. "Obviously, this is something I appreciate. I've seen all this since I was a child and of course I have special memories, but it's delightful that my wife loves it just as much and that she too can sense the mood."

Bold Interpretation

By the time the palace was ready for public display, the couple were anxious to move in. Everything turned out better than they had dared to hope. The Crown Prince calls the restoration's final stage extremely successful, not least because the modern art adorning the rooms makes the mansion manifest itself differently. "We've all had our visions, and the architectural drawings will chart a course, yet it's rare that the final result so thoroughly outshines the plans and visions. The modern art adds a new dimension, and it's been amazing to see the qualities of the old mansion blend with it so successfully."

Evaluating the final result, the Crown Prince can't help but wonder if some of the ideas will inspire others. "Perhaps this will show that there is no reason to be afraid to use modern art in older buildings. Unfortunately, not many private individuals have this opportunity, but it would be interesting to see other state buildings with public access embellished in a similar way."

Tradition and Innovation

The Crown Prince always knew that the palace would have contemporary art. The question was to which degree? From the onset, the available funds made it impossible for the palace to be decorated with works created specifically for the rooms. At that time, the Crown Prince's private art collection was intended for the walls. "We have a certain amount of modern art, which I have purchased in the USA over the past twelve or thirteen years, and I knew that those pictures would one day adorn our walls, but then came the opportunity to create customised works for the palace." The new works of art have become part of the palace and can't be removed, but that's not a concern of

Kathrine Ærtebjerg's decoration of
the pantry is inspired by its functions,
and the artist has painted a series of
hunting motifs.

the Crown Prince. He believes in the interaction between art and building. Tradition has, however, in certain cases been taken into consideration. "The banquet hall facing the Palace Square is preserved in the original shape and has been spiffed up with the colours they used back then."

In other instances, new paths have been taken, and though the Crown Prince is keenly aware of the scope of the remodelling and decoration, he has no misgivings. "It's the nature of man to be conservative and adverse to change, so naturally these drastic measures posed a challenge. We have crossed the borders into new territory, and not everyone is equally thrilled about what now hangs on the walls. But far more people than I had imagined were enthusiastic after visiting the palace. Not many pointed fingers and booed!"

Artistic Freedom

Naturally, he was curious to see what kind of works the artists would produce. "What will they be putting on the walls? I was excited to see that, and I did consider to what degree we should make recommendations. I believe that artists should be allowed to make their choices and not be disturbed. They prefer to be left alone." The Crown Prince and Crown Princess did ask the team of artists not to forget they were decorating an old house in close proximity to the maritime atmosphere of Copenhagen Harbour, and that the house was to be occupied by a young family. Those were the only and very general restrictions.

The artists produced sketches of how they imagined it should look. Then they began the work. "This has, as far as I know, been an exciting challenge to all of the artists involved. Because of the sizes of the surfaces, they had to paint directly on site and would not be working in the familiar surroundings of their studios. A few of them needed a little time to get used to that idea, but it took no more that a few brush strokes to make them comfortable with the situation. They entered into the spirit of the project and it became a good experience to work in this new and different environment. All of them were excited about the process."

Only one of the works was expelled, namely John Kørner's interpretation of the war in Afghanistan, but new attempts were made, and by the summer of 2010, the decoration drew to a close. Though the Crown Prince is evidently happy about these works of art, he refrains from appointing any favourites during his guided tour of the palace.

"It would be a shame to say thing like, 'this one is slightly better than that one'. They are all different and they all have different expressions, but all of them are actually extremely successful." In the opinion of some critics, the royal couple had been too bold in their reinterpretation and decorating, but this does not affect the Crown Prince. "Naturally there will always be someone who doesn't like parts of the decoration or who can't understand it. That's just how it is. I would rather have people say, 'I don't understand this one' or 'that one isn't very good' than to have everyone swoon." The works of art are not inconsequential. They point in many directions and indicate different paths. This will challenge the beholder and some works will not be to everyone's liking.

Artistic Interest

The Crown Prince is thrilled to be able to live in the presence of so many strong works of art. He can't point out the exact date when his interest in modern art emerged. It developed insidiously. "I've always been curious about art, and I've always been surrounded by my mother's paintings, although she doesn't do modern art as such. I have at times asked myself if I should give it a try, but then I let it pass. I don't think I have an artistic streak. I discovered instead that I could learn about art and get a better understanding of art." The Crown Prince started out with modern Danish art. Some of his friends are artists and collectors, and he knows gallery owners too. He has paid attention to the development of modern art and has gone to exhibitions to explore new works, even if he didn't always understand them at first glance.

The Crown Prince was soon drawn to the new generation of artists and he gradually developed a passion for and familiarity with contemporary art. He began buying art at auctions—"carefully and not too daringly"—and since then his interest has only grown deeper. He enjoys taking time to explore a work, but he also makes it clear that he is not a fan of wild and anarchistic art. "I like a certain amount of conformity. I have my limits, but even if at first I don't understand a specific work, I may understand it the next time, and I've found this to be an interesting process. Many things are not appealing at first, and that's how it should be. One has to make an effort to understand the work. It has to present a challenge."

His interest in art has deep roots in the family. The Queen and Prince Consort's interest in art is well known, and the same goes for Queen Ingrid who came from a Swedish family of talented painters. A work produced by one of the ancestors adorns a small chamber at Amalienborg. The picture shows dramatic and romantic scenery of mountains, forest and water. It's a staging of magnificent wilderness, bathed in heavenly light. "I like it. It's beautiful. It was the photography of the day. Perhaps it's the Scottish Highlands. He probably did a sketch on location and then went home and did the painting. A lot of people like a painting like this. The art of the Golden Age is incredibly beautiful, and while I do care about it, my imagination is more sparked by modern art." That's also the reason why the Crown Prince looks forward to witness his children growing up surrounded by such large-scale contemporary art.

"I look forward to asking my kids about what they see in these works of art. They may say to me: 'this is a tree, that is a stone, and over there is some water'. And that's just fine, because those kinds of answers are not wrong, and it would be just as fine for them to say that something looks like a cow turned upside-down, or whatever comes to mind. In modern art, you may have similar experiences while looking at a picture, or you may have completely different interpretations—and that fascinates me. And while the painting of the Scottish Highlands is beautiful and impressive, only an adult would look at it and say: 'Well, this composition is clear evidence that we are dealing here with the late Golden Age'."

The Parents' Reaction

Not surprisingly, the Crown Prince and Crown Princess were excited to see how the Queen and Prince Consort would react to the restoration of the palace, not least the new works of art. "We brought them over here at a time when a few of the artists had just finished their work. We wanted to see their reaction. Luckily, they were enthusiastic, and my mother expressed more and more enthusiasm as the work progressed." The Queen is especially fond of the ceiling painting by Eske Kath. "It's very beautiful because of the way he paints. I like his style, and I have a few other works by him, so I'm quite familiar with him. The way I see it, this painting is one of the most daring parts of the artistic embellishment, but when my mother saw it, she exclaimed: 'Wow, it's beautiful!' She thought it

Morten Schelde's mural in the reception chamber has disconnected objects from the past and the present floating in a surrealistic dream world. In this room, future visitors will wait for an audience with the regent.

sublime, which makes one very happy." The Queen has given the Crown Prince free rein. "Never at any time did my mother say: 'Please do be considerate—this is my childhood home!' Quite the contrary. She has paid attention, has gone over there with us and has been happy to see how it all has sprouted up."

The Crown Prince is aware of the fact that history repeats itself. He knows that his parents as newlyweds invited King Frederik and Queen Ingrid over when they had finished part of the decoration of the palace that would become their home. "Yes, I do remember my mother telling me about that. My parents used vivid colours, especially for the red salon, and she said: 'It was your father'. I believe he brought the inspiration with him from France where vivid colours are more accepted."

The Crown Prince respects the willingness of his parents to tread new paths and emphasizes his father's courage when it comes to challenging the conventions. He is well aware that it wasn't always easy and that he took some knocks, but the Crown Prince admires his father's attitude: "My father was criticized a lot when he married my mother. A lot of people thought he was strange and weird. He also broke with some of the conservatism that my grandmother and grandfather in his view represented. My grandfather was the patriarch, and his word was law. Then came my father with his Mediterranean ways, a southern European with his own style and taste and began making suggestion: 'Listen, how about doing things this way?' And that's what he did—not only at Amalienborg but also at Marselisborg, and the more I think about it, the more I believe he did the right thing. It's a very nice quality about my father. He is not contrary or argumentative just for the sake of it. Often he simply has a different approach to a discussion or an opinion, and I think that's healthy. In Denmark, we go by this Northern European style of consensus, and we are most at ease when we agree with everyone. And though that may be all right at times, it's healthy to see things from a new perspective and have a discussion. He has had always had the courage to do so and has dared to challenge the conventions."

Follow Your heart

Interview with Crown Princess

Along with Crown Prince Frederik, Crown Princess Mary has been in charge of a bold reinterpretation of Frederik VIII's Palace, the present workplace and home of the Crown Prince Couple.

New Year's Eve 2001, Mary Donaldson experienced the Danish royal family in full force for the first time. Unnoticed by the public, she had arrived in Denmark to celebrate New Year's with Crown Prince Frederik and his friends, and on that last evening of the year, Queen Margrethe would deliver her New Year's address to the nation.

Mary Donaldson was not aware of the importance of the speech, but as they got ready to broadcast directly from the Queen's study at Amalienborg, she could sense the intense atmosphere.

"I could see from people's faces that everyone was 100% present. All was quiet. Everybody was ready to listen. It was clear to me that I had better not say a word! It was momentous," she recalls.

When Queen Margrethe raised her eyes from the speech papers and began talking to the camera, the most important points were simultaneously translated for Mary, so she could understand the messages as they were delivered to hundreds of thousands of Danes who had gathered by the television sets in their homes to listen to the words of the regent.

The speech was followed by a moment of reflection and a discussion of the Queen's messages among the friends, and that is how the event has proceeded year after year, without losing any of its intimacy or meaning.

"Each year it's done in the exact same way. When the Guard marches in and the clock strikes, you are ready and hold a glass of champagne in your hand. It's a beautiful and strong tradition. It was the first I experienced, and it is one of my favourite traditions."

Since then, it has become, literally, a familial event. On May 14, 2004, she married the Crown Prince and joined the royal family as Her Royal Highness Crown Princess Mary Elizabeth.

To many Danes, however, she is quite simply Mary. Not disrespectfully so; it is more an expression of affection. Within the course of astoundingly few years, the Crown Princess has succeeded in bonding with her new country and new compatriots.

Growing up in Australia

The connection to Denmark was created in 2000, during the Olympic games in Australia. Mary Donaldson met the Danish Crown Prince at a party in Sydney. This meeting would not only establish a connection to the man she would marry, but also renew the ties to Europe that her family had left in the 1960s. The Crown Princess is the youngest daughter of John Dalgleish Donaldson, professor of applied mathematics, and Henrietta Clark Donaldson. The couple was married in Edinburgh in August 1963, and in November of the same year they emigrated to Australia.

The Donaldson's have four children; Jane Alison Stephens was born in 1965, Patricia Anne Bailey in 1968, John Stuart Donaldson in 1970, and Mary in 1972.

Mary has described family life as a close and happy one. After Hobart Matriculation College, where she got noted for her studies and her sports, she began, in 1989, her studies at the University of Tasmania where she graduated in 1994 with a Bachelor's degree in Commerce and Law. She moved to Melbourne to work for the advertising agencies DDB Needham and Mojo Partners. In 1998, she travelled in America and Europe, and had a several months' sojourn in Scotland where she worked for Rapp Collins Worldwide in Edinburgh.

She returned to Australia in 1999 and took a job as Account Director with Young and Rubicam, in Sydney, and stayed there until she was headhunted by another agency, and this career might very well have continued, but then something happened …

Successful Change of Scene

No one could have predicted that the transition from Australia to Denmark would turn out so successful. Today, however, it is evident that Mary, in her new role as Crown Princess, has helped cement an ancient monarchy's popularity. The Crown Princess' personality and appearance have from the outset made many sympathetic to her, and her unique significance to the Crown Prince Frederik has been evident to everyone. Many Danes recall the televised images from the wedding in Our Lady's Church, and how,

waiting at the alter, the Crown Prince had tears rolling down his cheeks. In her speech at the wedding, Queen Margrethe pointed out the Crown Princess' significance and defined the very moment the Crown Prince found his true self: "It happened when you met Mary. That's when it became spring in your mind, and everything blossomed around you."

Queen Ingrid

As a couple, Crown Princess Mary and Crown Prince Frederik have already been compared to Queen Ingrid and King Frederik. They exude the same harmony, and their internal division of roles resemble that of the previous and very popular royal couple. Like Queen Ingrid, the Crown Princess has become the wise life companion who has an eye for the opportunities and dangers of the monarchy at a time when having a royal family is not a matter of course. When Mary turned forty in February 2012, several historians ascertained the striking similarities between Crown Princess Mary and Queen Ingrid. "Both became crown princesses at a relatively young age, and both decided from the outset that they would go to great lengths in demonstrating their determination to become Danish." This was the assessment of the historian Lars Hovbakke Sørensen, who also emphasized the Crown Princess' involvement in community matters.

The historian Sebastian Olden-Jørgensen from the University of Copenhagen found the Crown Princess to have met expectations. "She meets any requirement the

Danes could possibly have. She is classy and knows how to talk to people, a gift that only to a limited degree can be taught. It's something you are born with, and the fact that Mary has this ability is a huge benefit for the royal family."

Several birthday portrayals mentioned the Crown Princess's willingness to always give more than her fair share. Secretary General of the Danish Refugee Council, Andreas Kamm, has witnessed the Crown Princess in operation. "She always gives more than has previously been agreed to with the Court. She will give more and longer interviews, and she will in general be available beyond what anyone could expect. It's highly admirable," says Andreas Kamm.

Overall, the shift from Australia to Denmark was executed with such grace that it is easy to forget the magnitude of the upheaval. In an interview with Berlingske Tidende for her fortieth birthday, the Crown Princess mentioned the effort involved with getting used to her new role as royal. Although she spoke of being on "a wonderful journey", the challenges must have been evident to the readers. "I felt very strongly that I had to prove my ability to live up to the expectations," said the Crown Princess.

The House

Looking back, the Crown Princess emphasizes that the transition to her new life in Denmark was cushioned by not having to move directly into Amalienborg. She and the Crown Prince began by moving into the Chancellery House at Fredensborg Palace. It made for a more gentle entrance, and the long, whitewashed and romantic house with direct access to the palace park, the woods and the lake became the setting of their first years as newlyweds.

"The Chancellery House is a house, whereas Amalienborg is a palace," says the Crown Princess. "It would no doubt have been more daunting if we had to move directly to Amalienborg. At Fredensborg you are protected by nature, and I felt comfortable from the moment I entered the house. It has warmth and atmosphere and felt like our own place." With Prince Christian born in 2005 and Princess Isabella in 2007, the royal couple had to get used to their new roles as parents and learn how to balance official duties and family life. It was a relief that they did not have to get used to these new roles in the more overwhelming and stately surroundings at Amalienborg. "Yes, you might call it fate, and these circumstances made the entry to my new life a bit easier."

Refurbishing the Palace

It was clear from the start, nonetheless, that the Crown Prince Couple would move into Frederik III's Palace, which had long since been chosen as the home and workplace of the future royal couple. The palace needed substantial renovation, and the Crown Prince Couple participated in every detail. The project soon turned into a bold reinterpretation of the edifice. "It has been an exciting project that began almost immediately after our wedding. The house had to be completely renovated, and in the process we also managed to turn it into our home. It was a big bite, but I think it worked out well," says the Crown Princess.

Along the way, the Chancellery House has served as inspiration, especially when it comes to creating a homey environment. "In the right wing of the building—and on the floors above—we have created our private section. It was a priority of ours that this should be one big apartment. In my childhood, we all slept in close proximity to each other, so our room and the children's rooms are all located on the mezzanine floor. We have created a bubble of our own where we gather as a family."

The last part of the décor, and the move itself, took place while the Crown Princess was very pregnant. In January 2011, she gave birth to the twins Prince Vincent and Princess Josephine, and these two youngest of their children are set to spend their entire childhood at Amalienborg.

Everyday Life

When the Crown Princess talks about the children, it is apparent that she wants to provide them with a childhood where family unity is more important than the delicate surroundings. "We both want to give our children all that we can, and we naturally want them to have a loving, caring and safe childhood, and for them to be happy. We want to be a family with an everyday life where we spend as much time together as possible."

The determination to not live in royal seclusion far away from the outside world is also evident when the Crown Princess makes her way about Copenhagen. "Official duties aside, I want to lead more or less the same life as other

women who live with husband and children. I ride out of the main gate with Isabella and see her to preschool. I jog at the citadel, take Ziggy for a walk, run errands and enjoy what the city has to offer. I also go to the movies, and sometimes have dinner in town."

The Crown Princess shares this outlook on life with Queen Margrethe, who has always emphasized that members of the royal family should be able to move around town without stopping traffic or causing a stir. "When I arrived in Denmark, I saw early photos of Queen Ingrid riding her bicycle around town. Fortunately, the ability of the members of the royal family to move around freely is an established tradition, and I believe the Danes still like it that way. There is no hullabaloo when I go to town, and I appreciate that. Some might look or say hello, but you are left in peace."

Palace Splendour

Conversely, the world inside the palace is infinitely far away from the reality outside. Several rooms have been furnished as reception rooms for guests of the Court, and these rooms show the palace in all its splendour. "Some rooms are furnished solely for entertainment, others have several features. The Great Hall is used for official events, but might also be the place where we celebrate Christmas. While expecting the twins, I couldn't move too far from the Copenhagen University Hospital so we set up a huge Christmas tree in the middle of the hall," says the Crown Princess.

A small doll stroller in a corner of the hall is a reminder that this room is being used—also by the little ones in the family. "Though the Great Hall is all about pomp and circumstance, it can be used in daily life as well," says the Crown Princess. She was involved in selecting the colour scheme, layout and furnishings of the imposing room, just as she has been involved with each of the other rooms in the palace. Light pours in from three tall palace windows and is reflected in mirrors. The Crown Princess is interested in photography and will sometimes take photos to try and catch the light that makes the room glow. Despite the lavish proportions, the room is surprisingly intimate. "The proportions are large and the room portentous, but it's still comfortable and has a good atmosphere," says the Crown Princess.

At the rear of the palace, another of the large reception rooms that face the gardens has been decorated with Gobelin traditional tapestries. It has, however, not yet been furnished as the couple allows themselves time to find the right decor and furnishings. Farther inside the building, she opens the doors to the Banquet Hall. The hall is located transversely and stretches across the entire width of the palace with windows facing the square and the gardens. A long mahogany table, originally a wedding gift to Crown Prince Frederik and Crown Princess Ingrid from the Swedish government, dominates the hall. The chairs, upholstered in light colours, offer a contrast to the dark tabletop that—for galas—will be with set with silver and decorated with flowers.

The Art in the Palace

The palace is imbued with modern art. "The easy and elegant character of the palace lends itself to contemporary art," says the Crown Princess. "The rococo style would have made this more difficult." Room after room display new works of art by talented young artists. Though the artists were given artistic freedom to decorate the palace, they did so in close dialogue with the Crown Prince Couple.

Inside the Crown Princess's study, previously Queen Ingrid's study, Erik A. Frandsen has created an oval-shaped medallion with a simple motif of three roses in a glass vase. The yellow petals are gracefully unfolding, creating life. The piece is composed of an astounding number of small marble pieces, applied to the wall in a thin layer. It took more than six hundred man-hours to place each sliver exactly right and polish the surface to its silky smoothness. "This is the jewel of the room," says the Crown Princess.

The room has modern Danish furniture classics: In front of the desk are two Arne Jacobsen Swan Chairs for guests, and there is a high back Arne Jacobsen office chair by the computer screen. The young designer, Cecilie Manz, has designed the desk. From this base, the Crown Princess works in close collaboration with her employees and Chamberlain Christian Schønau. The Crown Princess feels privileged to be able to work from home, but it raises the obvious question of how to maintain certain boundaries between work and leisure. Only a doorstep separates work from home—and vice versa. In other words, when is she at work and when is she home?

"It's a gray area, and one has to be careful not to let work take over completely, because it's so easy to just work all the time. When you're at home in your cosy surroundings and someone asks a work-related question, then the two worlds are not fenced apart. I believe one can always get better at keeping the two separate," says the Crown Princess.

On the other hand, having the office at the palace has obvious benefits. "The children can come and see me when I'm at the office, and it's nice that they're a part of it. 'What are you doing mom?' 'Come on, mom!' 'Do that later!' Sometimes I say, all right, here I come. At other times, I have to tell them I will be there shortly. It's a privilege not to have to commute back and forth between home and workplace. It saves many hours."

The Mary Foundation

The study is the place where she keeps track of the many activities she has become involved in. All year round she represents Denmark on official trips abroad, and in Denmark she frequently represents the Court at meetings with organizations, companies, and cities. During her first years, she was mostly known for marketing Danish fashion and design, but her patronage has increasingly focused on social issues, healthcare and humanitarian aid. She has, for instance, visited the famine-stricken areas near the Dadaab refugee camp in Kenya, and has, as patron of the Danish Refugee Council, visited refugee camps in Uganda to draw attention to the need for help.

At the suggestion of the United Nations Population

Fund, the Crown Princess, in 2012, became a member of an international panel that will fight maternal death, promote the health and rights of women, and bring about better access to family planning. In the developing countries, more than 220 million people are without access to modern family planning, and only half of the women in Sub-Saharan Africa give birth aided by a trained midwife. So help is imperative.

The Crown Princess' work is an extension of her involvement in the health and rights of women, and she has for quite some time addressed the conditions in the world's poorest countries. Presently, she is a patron of the United Nations Population Fund, Maternity Worldwide and the Danish Refugee Council.

In 2007, she took the biggest step in her professional life and established the Mary Foundation, which aims to combat social isolation, advance tolerance, promote the understanding of diversity, and create hope. The foundation identifies and implements projects in collaboration with organizations, foundations and experts.

"The Mary Foundation is structured differently from other foundations. We don't give away money but will explore, develop and run projects in collaboration with various partners," explains the Crown Princess. The purpose of the foundation is to combat social isolation, and that is no coincidence. It has, as the Crown Princess puts it, always been hard for her to see people be left out.

The foundation is based on the simple principle that everyone has a right to belong. "It makes me happy that I am happy to be able to help people who feel left out and to help them find their way into the community."

Three Focus Areas

The Foundation has three focus areas: Bullying, domestic violence, and loneliness. And although the Foundation has existed for only a short period of time, results have begun to show. The Foundation's first effort to stop bullying has introduced 120.000 children to the purple teddy bear, "Buddy Bear", who will comfort and encourage children while teaching them not to keep others out the play or out of the community. The programme has been implemented at a large number of preschools and schools in Denmark, and has also reached farther into the Danish Realm with "Buddy Bear" making his entrance in Greenland. The successful project—called "Free of Bullying"—has attracted international interest.

"It makes you happy to hear others tell you that the programme made a difference, that a child feels better, that someone is now showing new sides of themselves, or that the atmosphere in classroom has improved."

The campaign message is that bullying is unacceptable.

"Flowers. Fælledvej" is the title of Erik A. Frandsen's picture in the Crown Princess' study. It is made using the Scagliola technique, a complicated process where the coloured plaster-like Scagliola composite, placed in a carefully planned pattern, can be polished to resemble marble. Though the technique is old, it is characteristic of Erik A. Frandsen. Danish stucco worker Peter Funder and German specialist Manfred Siller have carried out the fine craftsmanship.

"We work to get everyone involved. It's not about putting a bullying child on display, since that child might have problems of its own. There is, in my opinion, no such thing as evil children. It's a task for professionals, parents, and children alike to make people aware that bullying is unacceptable and that everyone must help combat bullying. We now see children take responsibility and change their behaviour in class. It's a shift in culture, and that's why the effort against bullying should begin at an early stage."

Fighting bullying, teasing and harassment in the digital world, in cyberspace, is a new goal for the Crown Princess. "Computer games, the Internet and cell phones have, in almost no time, become part of the children's daily lives; yet they have not been taught how to behave in cyberspace. Non-digital ethics and values have not been adopted by the digital world. I often make the comparison that back when there were only few cars, it was not dangerous, but with more cars, rules are necessary to prevent accidents. The same applies to traffic in cyberspace. It can be a dangerous world, and we have to protect our children. It is important that the children learn the social rules on the Internet," says the Crown Princess.

Domestic violence

Another focus area is preventing and putting an end to domestic violence. It is a controversial topic that most people would rather ignore—and that is exactly why the Crown Princess wants to call attention to the abuse.

"There should be no violence, but there is, and we need to recognize this and respond," says the Crown Princess. Statistics show that 28.000 women experience domestic violence each year. Of these, 2.000 will seek help at shelters, but 26.000 battered women and their children receive little or no help. "It's important to help women, who live with violence, realize that it never is acceptable to live under those conditions. But merely focusing on it is not enough. They need tools that will enable them to get out of their situation. Some women stay in violent relationships for financial reasons, so we have established a project called "Advice for Life" to help women gain control of their finances and stand on their own two feet."

The work is hard. Many battered women are ashamed and will attempt to conceal the fact that they live with violent partners. "It's a long haul, but we know from the letters we receive that it means a lot to these women that someone listened to them."

The Crown Princess has met several of these women at shelters. "I need to understand how the spiral of violence works, so it's vital for me to speak with them directly. Some of these women were strong and had everything under control until they experienced violence."

The Crown Princess has also worked to increase awareness of battered women at an international level, and she often speaks at national as well as international conferences.

Loneliness

The third and most recent focus area of the Mary Foundation is loneliness. "It's a big and real problem in our society," says the Crown Princess. At the Mary Foundation's conference on loneliness, held at the Black Diamond extension to the Royal Danish Library in Copenhagen, one of the guest speakers was the American professor John T. Cacioppo, one of the world's leading loneliness researchers, and his speech made an impression.

He made the point that loneliness not only triggers mental or social pain, but that people become physically ill from loneliness. He said that people have been genetically coded to feel better when they are with other people. "John Cacioppo believes this dates back to a time when we had to stick together in order to survive. Once we are outside the community, things happen in our body. Deep inside we know that we are more vulnerable outside the circle. People who live alone will often have increased blood pressure, simply because they are on guard. Just as many people die from loneliness as from of obesity and smoking."

One thing in particular made an impression on the Crown Princess. In his speech, the professor mentioned how certain penguins survive the extreme cold of the Antarctic winters. "They share the middle circle, and have a method to ensure the survival of everyone. Those standing in the outer circle would perish if they had to stand only there all the time, and then the next circle would die, and the next after that until everyone had succumbed. So they take turns."

There is a lack of focus on loneliness as a research field, but the Crown Princess hopes to change that. When she, in December 2011, wrote a newsletter about the Mary Foundation's new focus area, the determination could not be mistaken. "The lonely need to know that many others are in the same situation. Let us not add pain and embarrassment to being lonely. It's difficult enough already."

A Genuine Commitment

The work of the Crown Princess has not only been noticed in Denmark.

In January 2013, she participated in the World Economic Forum's the annual meeting in Switzerland, along with heads of state and government, top international business executives, and leaders of humanitarian organisations.

Interestingly enough, she was present as one of the new members of Young Global Leaders, a network that is part of World Economic Forum. The invitation to join the group was based on her social commitment, especially the creation of the Mary Foundation.

She has, in her own quiet way, demonstrated leadership and has made results, and she makes no secret of how important it is for her to make a difference:

"We are in a privileged position and can create focus in areas that need attention. It's all about following one's heart. This has been my basis when selecting patronages and in establishing the Mary Foundation." She realizes that this kind of work depicts a royal family that, rather than merely ensconcing themselves behind the walls of Amalienborg, will reach out to society and engage in life outside. "That's how it is, and it has always been that way. But the effort will always mirror the person doing the work. You can't just play the part. It has to be a genuine commitment."

banquet requires lots of planning, and when the gaily decorated Amalienborg palace opens its doors for the expectant guests, this marks the end of months of preparations. A significant number of people with widely different duties have been involved, each and every one knowing exactly what task to perform.

The Master of Ceremonies

One of the main characters of this detailed planning is the Master of Ceremonies Christian Eugen-Olsen who ensures that everything is carried out according to protocol. The Master of Ceremonies has his office in the Yellow Palace in Amaliegade where he is usually occupied with the preparation of upcoming events, some of them large and involving many people, others more manageable in size. Prior to major parties he will write up a directive with detailed information on such things as: the number of guests attending, the required attire, how they will arrive, how they will be introduced, what to eat, what kind of entertainment, and when it all will be over. The Master of Ceremonies submits his ide-

DRESSED IN GALA

When the Court holds festive gatherings at Amalienborg, the event is always a display of pomp and circumstance, light and colours, and everything is characterized by a cheerful, yet ceremonious mood. Not least so when a banquet is being held in the Great Hall of Christian VII's Palace, which rightfully is regarded as Denmark's most beautiful and most precious Rococo interior. The Danish word for banquet—taffel—is an old German loan word that originally meant 'table', but in Danish the word has taken on different meanings and is exclusively used in connection with banquets held by the royal family on special occasions, such as birthdays, state visits—and the traditional New Year's Banquet for the government and prominent representatives of the official Denmark.

On all these occasion, traditions are observed and certain rules followed. Nothing is left to chance. A successful

as to the Queen who—being the host—makes the final decisions.

Military Precision

Christian Eugen-Olsen has been an officer for a long time, and when the royal family are scheduled to arrive at a destination, they will do so with military precision, on the dot, not one minute sooner or later. The same goes for the guests, who must arrive in a certain order, as determined by the protocol—the lowest rank first and the highest toward the end. If anything interferes with the sequence, the Master of Ceremonies can ask the police to hold back a specific car or ease another one through a busy intersection, and other things like that.

At large events, the Master of Ceremonies and all personnel on duty will convene fifteen minutes prior to the arrival of the first guests. He will discuss briefly with the Master of the Household and the adjutant any matters that need particular attention. Upon arrival, the royal family will bypass the royal chambers and get in position to receive the guests. And the Master of Ceremo-

nies will initiate the introductions. An adjutant will read each name aloud and thus offer the royal couple an opportunity to greet all of the guests, who will then go to their seats. After the introduction of the final guests, the royal couple will always be the last to take their seats.

From start to finish, the Master of Ceremonies and the Master of Household are in close cooperation. The Master of Household is responsible for the

practical things, such as making sure that the food and wine arrives at the right time and that the table is perfectly set with all place cards in the right spots.

Setting the table is a special challenge, and one Court functionary—or "taffeldækker"—has the overall responsibility. His three subordinates, the keepers of the silver plate, will set the tables in such a way that every glass, knife and fork is placed exactly right.

The ordinary duties of the keepers of the silver plate involves keeping up the silverware, glass and porcelain.

The Master of Household

When asked what's behind the rare title, the Master of Household (hoffourer, in Danish) Kenneth Madsen presents himself as kind of a butler to the royal family. It's his task—along with Chef de Cuisine Jesper Vollmer—to make sure the royal household is in good condition. In the old days, this was the servant in charge of procuring food, and in a way that's still the case, in a slightly extended sense. In times past, the Master of Household followed the regent on his travels to see to the condition of horses and carriages, and to ensure that accommodation was in order. Nowadays, the Master of Household will ensure that the royal residences are ready to receive the regent. This requires all the professional skills of the hospitality industry as well as overview and organizational talent.

Obviously, the Master of Household can't be everywhere at once, and the many tasks are delegated to the forty people who service the royal family. The Matron of the Household has her unique responsibilities, as does the Chef de Cuisine, and the chasseurs—a kind of foremen in charge of the daily service. The chasseurs attend to the Queen, while the footmen attend to the Prince Consort. The daily service team also includes a number of valets. The clothing of the employees is also the responsibility of the Master of Household, including valet uniforms and staff

attire for gala celebrations. An example of this would be the official banquet at a state visit, where a chasseur will stand behind the chair of the head of state, while a footman stands behind the partner of the head of state.

Prince Consort with Culinary Skills

The office of the Master of Ceremony at the Yellow Palace in Amaliegade is the heart of the busy Amalienborg work-

place. The Chef de Cuisine is responsible for the daily purchases of food, but the Prince Consort—perhaps due to his French background—has extensive gastronomic knowledge and takes a keen interest in the quality of the raw materials used in the kitchen and how they are cooked. For that reason he is usually in charge of the food and much the same could be said for the maintenance of the wine cellars of Amalienborg and Fredensborg. The Master of

Household takes care of the day-to-day purchases, but only after an exchange of professional opinions with the Prince Consort. It is often the characteristic, deep red, almost black Cahors wines from Prince's home region that will be served at the royal couple's dinner parties. That's the House Wine, served at all major events, while a small cellar at Rosenborg Palace stores the famous Rosenborg Wine—an old German Rhine wine, stored in barrels that are continuously replenished. Additionally, the royal family has a mobile wine cellar with younger wines that are not too fragile to be moved around the country, for example to the palaces of Gråsten and Marselisborg.

The Chef de Cuisine and the Master of Household will draw up menu suggestions for large gala dinners and then present these to the Prince Consort who will decide what will be served to the guests. A corps of waiters summoned for the occasion will serve at the banquet. They all have considerable professional serving experience, and the accidents that could happen when many people are gathered are few and minor. Kenneth Madsen will personally

ensure that the plan is followed to the letter and that the official speeches and selected pieces of music are executed according to schedule. The Band of the Royal Life Guards provides the table music. After one and a half hour, the Master of Household will usually find that the time has come to approach the Queen and say, "Your Majesty, I seek permission to close the royal banquet". After he has received his permission, he will go to a spot where the conductor can see him, and then, while the music plays, the Queen will signal by getting out of her chair. After this, the guests will take to the adjacent rooms for coffee and avec to be had while standing.

The Court Engine Room

For the Court to function optimally, and have each toothed wheel engage with the next, one entity has to gather all information and pass it on to the proper people. This takes place in the Court's engine room—the Lord Chamberlain's

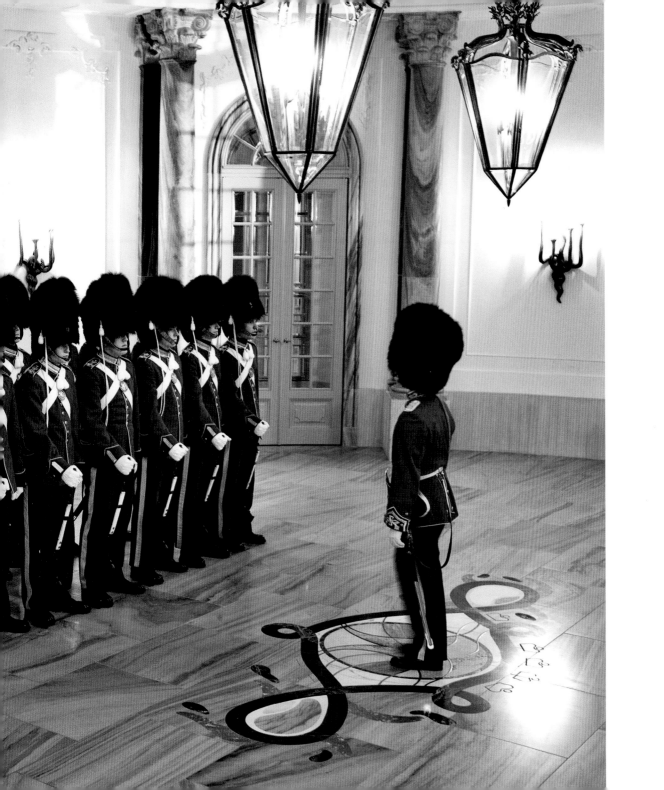

Office, or Secretariat—headed by Master of Law Astrid Ruge. As a member of the management group, she will work closely with the Lord Chamberlain and the Master of Ceremonies on upcoming big events, such as state visits. When a visit has been decided and entered into the calendar, preparations will begin and a task group of relevant collaborative partners, professionals and specialists will meet in the great hall of the Yellow Palace.

As the time of the visit comes closer, the Secretariat turns into something of a small manufacturing company. Guest lists and invitations must be prepared, and a program with all events scheduled by the minute. Other things to devise include driving and motorcade programs, accommodation plans, guest telephone lists, seating plans and place cards. All of this will be produced and printed at the Secretariat. A first draft of guest lists and seating plans will be sent to the Master of Ceremonies and the Lord Chamberlain before being submitted to the royals for final decision.

The Master of Household will regularly receive copies of the plans and it is his responsibility to make sure everything is executed as decided. "This sounds relatively simple, but a lot can go wrong," explains Astrid Ruge. If there is a sudden cancellation, the situation calls for a prompt response. The Danish Security and Intelligence Service need to be notified immediately, as does the airport and the driving coordinator. The Matron of The Household must also be informed, since the staff will not need to receive and accommodate the guest in question. The Master of Household must be advised in order to revise the seating plan, and the royals must be notified about any changes at their table.

During the COP 15 summit in December 2009, changes had to be made to the series of speeches, and on the Queen's 70th birthday celebration, the cloud of volcanic ash from Iceland had blocked air traffic. Though last minute changes were made on both occasions, everything was in order when the doors opened to the luminous ballroom at Amalienborg.

WINTERTIME

When the white frost settles on the square and the air is cold and clear, Amalienborg looks almost magical. On these occasions, the Queen is especially fond of looking across the square. But even during the harshest blizzard, the magic remains. All year round and at any time of day, Amalienborg has that special glow. The Queen and Prince Consort will stay at Amalienborg Palace all winter, except for Christmas when they relocate to Marselisborg Palace.

Amalienborg

© 2013 Jørgen Larsen, Thomas Larsen, Bjarke Ørsted
& Gyldendal Publishers, Denmark
Text©: Jørgen Larsen og Thomas Larsen
Photos©: Bjarke Ørsted
Graphic design: Janus René Andersen
Text type: Palatino and Grotesque
Printed and bound by Ednas Print in 2013

ISBN 978-87-02-12438-5
10 9 8 7 6 5 4 3 2 1